EALING, ACTON & SOUTHALL AT WAR

EALING, ACTON & SOUTHALL AT WAR

DENNIS UPTON

This book is dedicated to my dear parents John Stanley Upton and Eleanor Upton and to all the other men and women of their generation who fought the good fight in the Second World War.

Frontispiece: Mr Heard sitting amongst the ruins of his home in Westfield Road.

First published 2005
This edition published 2009

The History Press
The Mill, Brimscombe Port
Stroud, Gloucestershire, GL5 2QG
www.thehistorypress.co.uk

British Library Cataloguing in Publication Data.
A catalogue record for this book is available from the British Library.

ISBN 978 0 7524 4954 8

Typesetting and origination by The History Press
Printed in Great Britain

CONTENTS

Foreword 6

Acknowledgements 7

Bibliography 8

Introduction 9

A UK wartime calendar: 1939-45 10

one   Preparations and countdown to war: 13
1926-39

two   From declaration of war to Dunkirk 19
evacuation: 1939-40

three   Air attacks on Britain and the impact on 27
Ealing, Acton and Southall: 1940-45

four   Personal recollections of life under fire 67

five   Victory days and nights: 1945 77

six   A miscellany of wartime facts and figures 87

Glossary: A wartime alphabet 115

Afterword 121

Index 124

FOREWORD

I am very pleased to recommend this addition to the history of the London Borough of Ealing. I hope that it will encourage people to look back on the contribution made by so many residents of the borough during those years of hardship and trial.

Councillor Ian M. Potts,
Mayor of the London Borough of Ealing, 2005

ACKNOWLEDGEMENTS

I would like to thank Dr Peter Hounsell of the London Borough of Ealing Central Library and, particularly, the staff of the Local History Centre for their support in this venture. My especial thanks go to Dr Jonathan Oates for his ready advice and help in providing much of the basic material for my book.

I am also indebted to West London & Bucks Newspapers Ltd and to several editors of the *Ealing Gazette* and its sister newspapers for permission to use some of the wartime photographs, features and articles from the *Middlesex County Times*.

My thanks go also to Mrs Hilary Potts who, in an exceedingly busy year as Mayoress of the London Borough of Ealing, has not only dealt with the typescript so efficiently, but who has also supplied good source material through her many personal contacts in the borough, her membership of the Questors Playback team and her internet skills.

I acknowledge too the contributions of those people who, through their private journals or written responses to local newspapers, websites and history groups, have helped to illuminate this wartime story. Their names will be found in the text of my book.

BIBLIOGRAPHY

The HMSO official war histories have provided most of the background information on the national scene. Information on local events has been largely obtained from unpublished diaries, Home Office files in the Public Records Office, individual responses, written and oral, local newspaper and history publications.

AEC, *Contribution to Victory*, Adams & Shardlow, 1947

Bartlett, Roy, *A little boy's War*, New Millennium, 2002

BBC WWII 'People's War' website (bbc.co.uk/dna/ww2), 'Memories of Ealing' website (www.lammas.com)

Calder, Angus, *The People's War*, Jonathan Cape, 1969

Fitzmaurice, Paul, *Little Ealing, a walk through history*, Ealing Fields Residents' Association, 2002

Graves, Charles, *London Transport at War*, Almark Publishing, 1974

Harrisson, Tom, *Living through the Blitz*, Collins, 1976

Hoover, *From Peace through War to Victory*, Hoover Ltd, 1946

McAlpine, Sue, *Voices of Ealing and Hounslow*, Tempus Publishing, 2000

Meads, R.J., *Southall: 1830-1982*, (Braunton) Merlin, 1983

O'Brien, T.H., *Civil Defence*, HMSO, 1955

Price, Alfred, *Blitz on Britain*, PBS, 1976

Radcliffe, Sir Clifford, *Middlesex* (New Ed.), Evans Bros, 1954

Scouse, F.W. (ed.), *Ealing, 1901-1951; Souvenir to commemorate the jubilee of Ealing Corporation*, June 3 1951,

Simpson, Ian and Wilcox, John: *The Northolt Story*; 85th anniversary edition, RAF Northolt, 2001

Titmuss, R.M., *Problems of Social Policy*, HMSO, 1950

Wallis, C.R., *Ealing at War*, chapter 9 'Festival of Britain', Ealing Borough Council Public Relations Committee, 1951

Wood, Derek & Derek Dempster, *The Narrow Margin*, Arrow Books, 1967

INTRODUCTION

Some readers may possess or recall a book by the same author and on the same subject which appeared in 1993. That book, *The Dangerous Years*, was limited in scope and print run and is long out of print. This book is a much enlarged version of the original and contains more photographs, more personal reminiscences and more general information on those eventful years. It also contains extracts from the wartime diaries and books compiled by local people.

Additionally, this book appears at a most appropriate time – in the year which sees the sixtieth anniversary of the victorious conclusion of the Second World War. The review is in several parts, and places local events in their national context. Official records, reports, war histories, websites and, not least, local newspapers have provided much of the background material. The book covers the preparation for and countdown to war; the outbreak of war, the air attacks on the (then) three boroughs of Ealing, Acton and Southall and many other aspects of wartime life.

This account will, I think, stir the memories of older readers, surprise younger readers and could stimulate interest in our local history amongst newcomers to the district. It may also provide the answers to some long-standing questions as to what did happen locally.

Finally, I hope that my book will be seen as a valuable addition to the recorded history of our district.

Dennis Upton,
Ealing, 2005

A UK WARTIME CALENDAR: 1939-45

1939

31 March	Britain's pledge to Poland; 'aid at once' if attacked by Germany
1 September	Germans invade Poland. Evacuation begins
3 September	War declared at 11.00 a.m. by the Prime Minister, Neville Chamberlain, and by France at 5.00 p.m. First air-raid warning sounded – a false one
16 October	First air raid, on British warships in the Firth of Forth
17 October	First bombs dropped on British soil – falling on the Orkney Islands
9 December	First British soldier killed in action

1940

January	Food rationing introduced
16 March	First civilian killed by enemy action – in Orkney
9 May	First bombs dropped on the mainland – in Kent
3 June	Dunkirk evacuation completed
10 June	Italy declares war on Britain and France
14 June	Paris falls
22 June	French armistice with Germany and Italy
30 June	Channel Islands occupied. A second wave of evacuation from London begins
10 July	Battle of Britain begins
24 August	First bombs dropped on London
26 August	First all-night raid on London
7 September	'Blitz' on London begins, followed by first bombs to be dropped on Ealing, Acton and Southall
29 December	Fire raid. The City of London burns

1941

10 May	Heaviest bombing raid on London – end of 'The Blitz'
1 June	Clothes rationing begins
22 June	Germans invade the Soviet Union
7 December	Japanese attack Pearl Harbour
8 December	Britain and the USA declare war on Japan and the USA on Germany and Italy.

1942

15 February	Singapore falls to the Japanese
8 March	Rangoon falls
3 November	Victory at El Alamein over the Germans and Italians, followed by German retreat in the Western Desert.

1943

31 January	Germans surrender at Stalingrad
13 April	Germans surrender in Tunisia
5 July	Sicily invaded by Allies
8 September	Italy surrenders.

1944

31 January	First 'Little Blitz' attack on London in series
6 June	D-Day: Invasion of European mainland
13 June	V1 flying bomb onslaught on South East England begins, followed by a third evacuation wave from London and the South East
8 September	First V2 rockets on Chiswick and Epping

1945

27 March	Last V2 rocket on UK (Orpington)
29 March	Last V1 dropped in Hertfordshire. (Last local one on Greenford on 14 March)
8 May	VE Day. Germany surrenders
9 May	Channel Islands liberated
3 July	General Election; Labour landslide. Clement Attlee replaces Winston Churchill as Prime Minister
5 August	Atomic bomb dropped on Hiroshima
8 August	Soviet Union declares war on Japan
9 August	Atomic bomb dropped on Nagasaki
14 August	Japan Surrenders
15 August	VJ Day

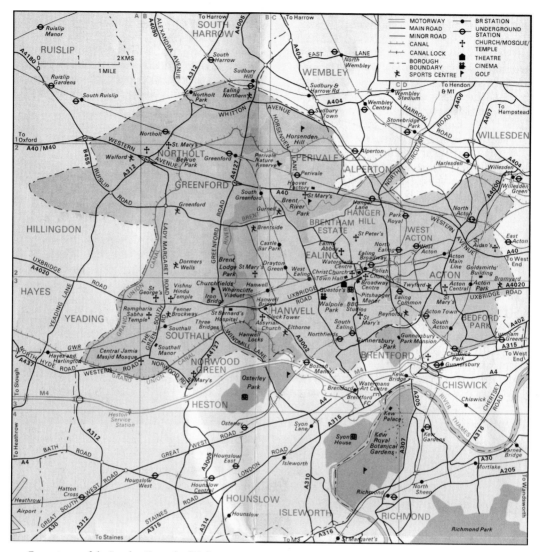

Current map of the London Borough of Ealing.

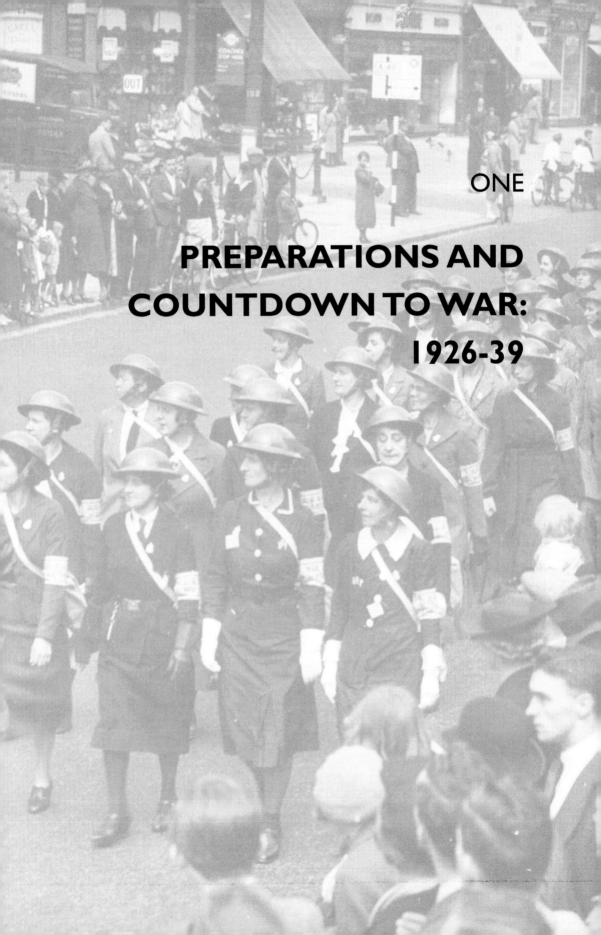

ONE

PREPARATIONS AND COUNTDOWN TO WAR: 1926-39

One cannot, of course, describe the impact of the Second World War on our local area without referring to the pre-war years and so national and, indeed, international events will feature largely in this section.

On 28 June 1919, at Versailles, Marshal Foch, the French military leader, turned to his colleagues and said, 'This is not peace, it is an armistice for twenty years.' His sense of foreboding had arisen on reading the peace terms agreed by the Germans in the Treaty of Versailles – terms which inflicted on the defeated Germans severe territorial losses, large financial reparations and very restricted armed forces. Sadly, Marshal Foch's fears were to be realised – almost to the day.

The impact of the First World War of 1914-18 was devastating, not so much in terms of physical destruction as in the human losses suffered by the combatants. The Great War, as it came to be known in public sentiment, was 'the war to end all wars,' but public hopes were not to be realised. The grim aftermath of the war with bankruptcies, massive unemployment and starvation spawned fascism in Italy and Germany and communism in Russia and, in Germany, nationalism was fuelled by cries for revenge.

By the mid-twenties, the need for maintaining and, if necessary, increasing national military and civil defences was being argued in the political assemblies of Europe. In Britain, the emphasis was more on civilian defences – the air attacks of 1915-18 having greatly shocked the British people. In these air raids, the British had seen and felt the physical presence of an enemy on their island after an interval of nearly 900 years. The raids themselves, compared with those of the Second World War, had not been unduly heavy. The fifty-one raids by airships (Zeppelins) had killed 558 civilians and injured 1,385 and a further sixty-three raids by aircraft (Gothas and Giants) on London and south-east England had added 857 more dead and 1,982 injured to the total. The damage caused was not extensive but the very novelty of aerial attack had produced a reaction out of all proportion to the damage and casualties sustained. Discussion on aerial attacks and means of defence did not end with the war in 1918.

By 1926, the term Air Raid Precautions (ARP) was in use and a voluntary scheme of ARP wardens (similar to the Special Constables recruited during the General Strike of 1926) was envisaged. But there were difficulties in a voluntary scheme – in the very nature of things, the volunteers in those days tended to come from the middle classes, for example, areas like Ealing, and this did not augur well for the more vulnerable, densely populated, working-class areas.

In January 1933, Adolf Hitler and his National Socialist (Nazi) Party assumed power in Germany and, in October of the same year, Hitler held his first Nuremberg rally at which he spoke of German revenge for Versailles and of the need for German expansion. A chill went through Europe and in Britain thoughts turned increasingly to the defence of the country and to rearmament. In the civil defence field, discussions on the evacuation of London and other, vulnerable big cities took place and it was estimated that 3,500,000 people would have to be

Before the bombs fell, Ealing Broadway, 1937.

evacuated from London alone. It was also agreed that 'black-out' precautions (first imposed in the First World War) would have to cover the whole of the UK. The fears of instant, massive and continuous enemy air attacks and the use of poisonous gases against the civilian population cannot be exaggerated and were the keynote to all 'official' thinking on the subject in the thirties and so, in 1934, it was agreed that the whole population should be issued with (anti) gas masks, if the political situation worsened.

The first circular to local authorities – including Ealing, Acton and Southall – was issued in July 1935, and this led to ARP committees being set up in all the larger cities and towns at the request of the government and a series of meetings on anti-gas measures with representatives of local authorities followed. The Observer Corps of volunteer, civilian aircraft spotters was placed under the Air Ministry and the vital radar cover of the eastern and southern approaches to Britain was established from 1935 onwards. 1936 saw the plans for gas-mask distribution agreed and production of the civilian gas mask began at a new factory in Lancashire. Air-raid warning districts were created, based on telephone exchange areas, and the ARP messenger service, first undertaken by members of the Boy Scouts Association, was opened up to volunteers from the general ranks of young people. In April 1937, the Air Raid Wardens' Service was introduced (still almost entirely voluntary); in May, Neville Chamberlain succeeded Stanley Baldwin as Prime Minister; in July, the government voted a further £1 million towards the production of civilian gas masks, and the training of police and local government employees in anti-gas measures began in earnest.

The 1930s had seen a quickening in civil defence activity but still with no great sense of urgency. But events in 1938 were to change all that.

1938: The national scene

1938 was a year of great events and of deep emotion – a year when war seemed imminent and then peace seemed secured. Fear was replaced by joy, and, then, relief was followed by nagging doubts and, with hindsight, one can see that the countdown to war had begun.

In January, Regional Offices of the ARP were established in Britain; in March, Hitler seized Austria and demanded the return of the German population in the Czech border areas. In August, Chamberlain made the first of a number of flights to negotiate with Hitler. Air-raid trenches were dug in the public parks of British cities and the distribution of gas masks for the civilian population began in September. On 30 September, Chamberlain returned to Heston aerodrome from his meeting with Hitler in Munich and bore with him the piece of paper, signed by the Nazi leader, which was supposed to be the guarantee of peace in Europe. The Prime Minister was cheered at Heston and in the House. He was thanked by the King and received thousands of letters and gifts from all over the world, for the sense of deliverance was not confined to Britain. But many saw the Munich deal as a humiliating surrender and the sense of euphoria diminished rapidly. Rearmament proceeded apace, and aircraft production, for example, trebled within twelve months of Munich and included the vital Hurricane and Spitfire fighters. The distribution of Anderson shelters (named after the designer Dr David Anderson) began in the winter of 1938 and brick street shelters appeared. Sales of the record *God bless you, Mr Chamberlain* slumped, and, by Christmas 1938, the optimism of autumn had been replaced by a feeling that war with Nazi Germany had only been postponed.

The local scene

The Ealing edition of the *Middlesex County Times* of Saturday 1 October 1938 highlighted the great efforts made in the preceding week in the field of civil defence. 124,000 gas masks had been distributed from depots set up in schools, hospitals and the Town Hall and all available labour, including the unemployed, had been used to dig trenches in the parks, open spaces and school playgrounds. The Medical Officer of Health was urgently installing first-aid posts throughout the borough of Ealing and similar activities were also taking place in Acton and Southall.

Two telegrams referred to in the newspaper best reflect that anxious last week of September 1938 – one expressing great relief, and the second far less optimistic in tone. The first telegram was from the Mayor of Ealing, Cllr J. Mansel Lewis, to the Prime Minister, Mr Chamberlain, and read: 'The inhabitants of Ealing thank you for saving the peace of Europe. Their hearts are full of the deepest gratitude. Their admiration of your diplomacy, courage and perseverance is intense.' (It should be noted here that cables couched in similar words were received by the thousand at No.10 Downing Street from every corner of the country and the Empire.)

The second telegram was received in the Town Hall from the Home Office on Friday 30 September – the day of the Munich agreement. This instructed the Council to continue the distribution of gas masks and promised to supply protective cartons for them. The population, it stressed, should be warned of the need for taking great care of their respirators (gas masks). It also advised that whilst no new trenches should be dug, existing ones were to be made good against collapse and bad weather and were not to be filled in.

These two telegrams summed up the ambivalence felt in those autumnal days of 1938 – relief that war had been averted coupled with a determination to continue with measures to protect the civilian population in the event of war.

Regarding the Mayor of Ealing's telegram, it should be recorded that not all Ealing inhabitants shared the Mayor's wholehearted approval of the Munich agreement. One resident, Mr A.K. Goodlet, a keen observer of the political scene and a strongly opinionated gentleman, was clearly prescient when he wrote in his journal as follows:

10/9/38. The Sudeten (Czech) problem is being solely used by Germany to exert pressure in what is only one step in a deliberate campaign to overrun and dominate Europe …these factors call

Digging ARP trenches in Walpole Park, 1938.

on us to stand firm and to proclaim an end to this (German) policy of brutal force and wanton illegality.

There followed meetings between Mr Chamberlain and Hitler and of these two with the French and Italian leaders. Czechoslovakia was dismembered and, in effect, war had begun.

Mr Goodlet's comments on the agreed Munich terms were harsh: "To me it seems a complete surrender to Hitler and a humiliating final desertion of the Czechs and of the principles for which we have been standing out... What a humiliation! But I suppose it means peace – for how long?" Mr Goodlet was, however, in a small minority. There was a palpable sense of relief in the three boroughs as throughout Britain.

Air Raid Precautions speeded up from the Munich agreement until the outbreak of war in September 1939. Government plans for evacuation were published and Acton, and that part of Ealing and Hanwell south of the Great Western Railway line, were amongst the evacuable areas. The rest of Ealing and Southall were deemed 'neutral' areas, that is, they were not evacuable but also were not reception areas for evacuees.

1939: The national scene

In March 1939, the Germans, in violation of the Munich agreement, seized the rest of Czechoslovakia and increased their violent threats against Poland. The British, convinced now that war was almost inevitable, guaranteed the territorial integrity of Poland in conjunction with the French. The die was now cast.

In Britain, the build-up of the ARP services proceeded apace. The basic unit of civil defence was the Wardens' post, manned by three to six wardens and responsible for an average of 500 residents per post (occasionally many more than this). The wardens, men and women, were the backbone of the ARP service, and, in 1939, only 16,000 of London's 200,000 wardens were full-time, paid personnel. The ARP system consisted of the Group HQ, covering several boroughs; then the Borough HQ, each with its Report and Control Centre (usually in the Town Hall) and then the District Control, with up to 10,000 people in each District. The ARP hierarchy consisted of the Chief Warden, District Wardens, Post Wardens, Senior Wardens and Wardens, and, by September 1939, the national strength of the ARP organisation had reached 1,500,000. Of these, 1,100,000 were part-time, voluntary personnel and one in six, or 250,000, were women. Most of the women wardens were part-time, were predominantly middle-aged or elderly and, naturally, tended to reflect the social characteristics of their neighbourhoods. The Rescue teams consisted in the main of peace-time building workers who were called upon to apply their skills in reverse when the raids began; pulling down and dismantling buildings and digging people out.

In Europe, the Germans completed their plans for the invasion of Poland in June 1939 and began massing their forces on the long Polish frontier.

By the summer of 1939, preparations for war were continuing apace. More trenches were dug (including schools) and Anderson shelters provided for householders with gardens in evacuation and neutral areas, like Ealing, Acton and Southall. In August of that year, the streets of the three boroughs were a strange sight with sandbags protecting important buildings, including the Town Halls. The tops of Post Office pillar boxes were given a coating of gas detector paint (fear of gas attacks was most acute); local gas identification squads were recruited from qualified chemists; decontamination squads from street cleaners, 'Mickey Mouse' gas masks were issued to children and gas helmets for babies into which the mother pumped air by means of bellows. Additionally, to deal with the large number of casualties expected, many cars and vans were confiscated for use as ambulances and, chillingly, a large number of shrouds and papier-mâché coffins were ordered. On 9 August a trial 'black-out' was held in the three boroughs and on 24 August reservists could be seen responding to the 'call-up' and the ARP services were put on alert.

ARP – women volunteers, parade on Ealing Broadway, July 1939.

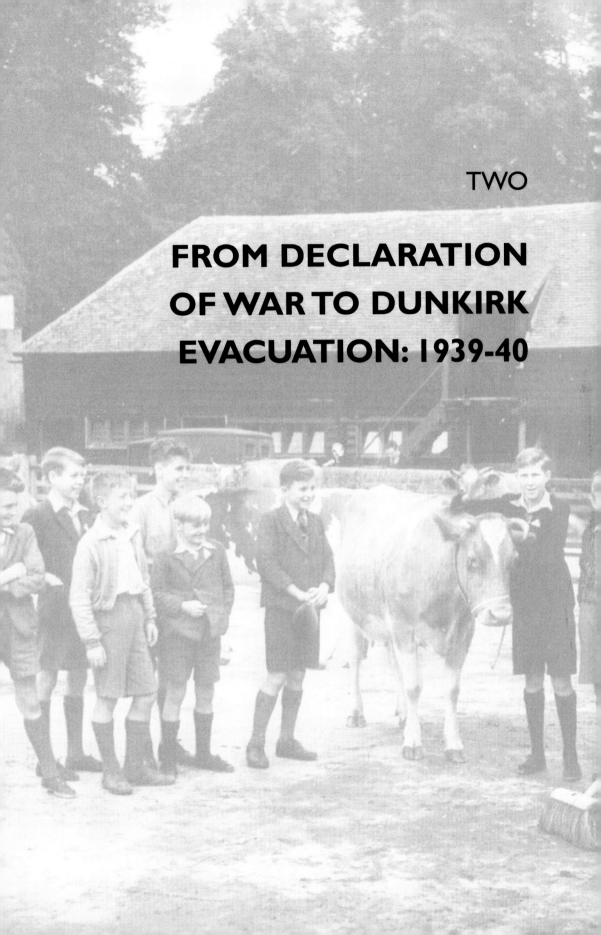

TWO

FROM DECLARATION OF WAR TO DUNKIRK EVACUATION: 1939-40

The Germans invaded Poland on Friday 1 September, and, on the same day, the evacuation of children and nursing mothers began from the big cities in Britain and the official blackout was imposed at sunset.

The British and French ultimatum to Germany, demanding the withdrawal of her forces from Poland, expired on Sunday 3 September, and at 11.00 a.m. on that fateful morning, the Prime Minister broadcast the British declaration of war. Mr Chamberlain's voice sounded tired and infinitely sad when, within a few minutes of the end of his speech, the air-raid sirens wailed. It seemed as though London was about to experience once more the horrors of aerial bombardment. The air-raid warning was a false one, however, and bombs would not fall on the capital for many months.

Local, personal reactions to the declaration of war varied from calm acceptance to great anxiety and grief. A.K. Goodlet (now working for the Port of London Authority River Emergency Service) had come off night duty at Cadogan Pier that morning and his rest was disturbed as follows:

I heard in my sleep with incredulity the sirens giving the air-raid warning. Woke at length and realised the authorities would not indulge in practice alarms and that this must be the real thing. Piled on clothes faster than ever and rushed to my station where I found everyone taking it very calmly, as it appeared to be merely a sort of official confirmation of the speech a few minutes earlier by Mr Chamberlain (declaring war).

Roy Bartlett, then aged nine and living with his parents in South Ealing, describes the family's reaction in his book, *A Little Boy's War*:

The Prime Minister eventually (the broadcast had been delayed by fifteen minutes) spoke in tremulous tones as millions hung on his every word, concluding, 'No such undertaking has been received, therefore, I have to tell you that this country is at war with Germany.' Mum had sat with her arm around my shoulders during the broadcast and I felt her stiffen as the family sat stunned by the news, however much this was expected. Dad finally broke the tension as he quietly said, 'Oh well, that's it. Better get on with it now I suppose.'

The sirens wailed and the family listened intently for the sound of enemy aeroplane engines but, '…all remained quiet until the silence was broken by someone shouting in the street, followed by a clatter against our front door. Some poor lady, overcome by the situation had chosen our doorway to throw a faint!'

The local scene

Let us switch now to the general impact of those momentous days on the three boroughs, bearing in mind that Ealing incorporated Hanwell, Greenford, Perivale and Northolt in its boundaries. The *Middlesex County Times* of Saturday 2 September 1939 announced that Ealing was ready for any emergency, and reported the following: 100,000 sand-bags had been placed against the walls of King Edward Memorial Hospital to protect the hospital from bomb blast and splinters, and other buildings were being protected similarly; 50,000 children from West London had been entrained at Ealing Broadway Station on Friday 1 September, and had been despatched to safety in the West Country; Ealing schoolchildren from the area south of the GWR line would follow, and anti-gas helmets for babies would be available shortly. There was a large increase in the number of marriages and (it would seem) an increase in suicides. Yet day and half-day trips were still being advertised to Dublin (22/6), Glasgow (27/9), Liverpool (11/-), and Birmingham (6/9) and a gentleman from Hampstead had been charged at Ealing Police Court with being drunk and incapable in Hanger Lane. It was said that,'…each time a row of traffic accumulated at the traffic lights, the accused caused an obstruction with his umbrella.' For the record, it must be said that the gentleman was not Mr Chamberlain, temporarily unhinged by the failure of his peace efforts, and in any event the case was dismissed.

One week later, in the 9 September edition, there was a reference to the first air-raid warnings of the war (all false); to the evacuation of Ealing schoolchildren in London Transport buses to Buckinghamshire, Berkshire, and Oxfordshire, and to the holiday atmosphere prevailing amongst the evacuees. The 16 September edition said that some 4,000 children and adults had left Ealing and had been visited by the Mayor, Alderman Mrs Taylor; that the blackout was causing

Evacuees leaving from Ealing Broadway station, 1 September 1939.

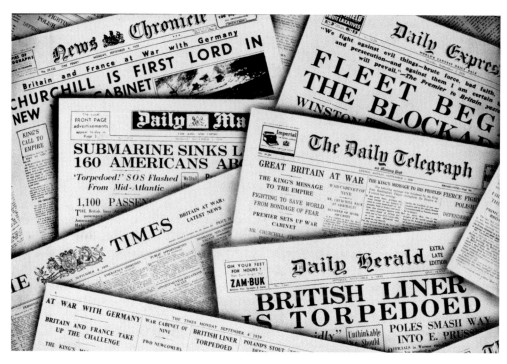

Fleet Street headlines, Monday 4 September 1939.

Evacuation party from Bordeston Boys' School, Hanwell, 3 September 1939.

Evacuation party from Bordeston Boys' School, down on the farm.

many more accidents; that cinemas and theatres, closed on the outbreak of war, had re-opened on the fifteenth, but that programmes must end by 10.00 p.m. The number of evacuees from inner London, handled at Ealing Broadway station had passed the 100,000 mark and deep underground air-raid shelters were being constructed on Haven Green and in Dean Gardens.

Much activity was also to be found in Acton. The *Acton Gazette & West London Post* in its Friday 8 September edition reported the evacuation of large numbers of schoolchildren and mothers with younger children from Acton Central Station (GWR) to Dorset and Devon. Nearly 1,000 men were said to have besieged the nearest recruiting office during the week and hundreds of young couples had flocked to the principal registry offices in London to get married at the earliest opportunity. Dozens of people had volunteered to fill sandbags to protect hospitals and other public buildings; twenty-nine permanent ARP posts had been constructed and trenches were to be dug on Acton Green with minimum delay. The paper also paid tribute to the calm way in which the first air-raid warning had been received – particularly by crowds of children about to board a train for safety. Actonians were also advised that, 'this country has never been better protected (from air attack)' – a statement not borne out by the heavy raids of 1940.

And for Southall readers, too, a similar picture – of praise for the disciplined reaction to the first air-raid warnings; for the state of readiness of the local ARP and other civil defences, for the volunteer fillers of sandbags and for the gearing up of the local industries to the war effort. (Later, in June 1940, Southall was hit by an evacuation tragedy when the SS *City of Benares*, which was carrying evacuees to the United States, was torpedoed and sunk. Four Southall children were amongst the victims. This sinking brought the official overseas evacuation scheme to an end.)

A note on evacuation – arguably the greatest social upheaval in our history – would be timely at this stage. There were three main waves of evacuation from London – in September 1939; the summer and autumn of 1940 and during the flying bomb onslaught in the summer of 1944.

WHO SAID WE'RE UNHAPPY ?

Right: *A newspaper cutting captures the smiling faces of Acton Wells Infants' School evacuees in Devon, 1939.*

Opposite: *Polish émigré minister at University College Hall, Ealing, with Polish refugees, 1940.*

The schemes, voluntary except in the case of homes for the aged and disabled and for certain hospital patients, produced an uneven response. Generally, the poorer the district, the poorer the response and the greater the reluctance of mothers to part with their children. A Cambridge evacuation survey in 1941 emphasised the fears of the mother of the evacuated child whose affections might be transferred to its new foster mother:

> Among the simple and the poor, where there is no wealth, no pride of status or possessions, love for the members of one's own family and joy in their bodily presence alone makes life worth living. So deeply rooted is this need that it has defied even the law of self-preservation, as well as urgent public appeals and the wishes of authority.

The impact on the evacuated child, starved of parental love, could also be deleterious, 'For without affection, life has little meaning for most people and none at all for children.'

The young Roy Bartlett lived and went to school (Little Ealing) in the evacuation zone of Ealing. Supported by his family he had no desire to become an evacuee until he realised that he was the only one in his class not going and quickly decided to go along with his best friend. His adventures continue after the following extracts from the Little Ealing School log, which appears in the book, *Little Ealing, a walk through history*:

> Three weeks before the end of the summer term in 1939 it was announced that 270 children were to be evacuated to Buckinghamshire. The junior school children (7 to 11 years) went to Bourne End and the senior boys (11+) and infants (5 to 7 years) to Woburn Green. The evacuees were encouraged by the kind welcome they received. The children were taught in shifts, sharing premises with local schools. Their free time was used for activities such as nature study and organised games. However, the number of evacuated children declined as parents

brought them home and by February 1941 only eighty remained. Quite a large number of children remained in Ealing throughout the war years. Little Ealing School reopened in 1940 to cater for children from the surrounding area, some of whom had attended other schools. Air raids constantly interrupted the school day and staff had to take turns in fire watching at night (from January 1941). School holidays were curtailed to keep schools open and, generally, everyone was under a great deal of strain. School meals were introduced at Little Ealing for the first time in 1942.

Roy Bartlett's situation was eased somewhat when his best friend's mother was co-opted as a helper and undertook to get the two boys billeted together. He describes in his book the assembly, departure and arrival of his group of evacuees:

> We all assembled with increasing excitement and trepidation as emotional goodbyes were said all around. Tears flowed profusely as mums cried out, 'Don't forget to write – be good – wash behind your ears' and all the other platitudes that mothers are famed for. Having been tagged with large labels proclaiming our name and school we clambered aboard London double-decker buses…

Roy and his friend were very fortunate to be picked out in the village hall by 'a kindly smiling couple… so commenced a friendship with Connie and Bill that was to last more than sixty years and turn full cycle when Bill became godfather to my own son.' A heartening story and a tribute to the kindly couple and to Roy, who returned home in May 1940.

Further afield, the news was not so reassuring. Warsaw surrendered on 27 September 1939 after a heroic stand, and organized, military resistance ended in Poland. On the Western Front, activity was restricted to patrols and the occasional exchange of shells, and London and Paris

remained unbombed. The only warfare activity was at sea where a grim struggle had begun against German U-boats and mines which were taking a deadly toll of Allied shipping.

It was the time of the 'phoney' war and, at home, the main civilian preoccupations were coping with separation from loved ones, the black-out, growing food shortages and with the very severe winter of 1939-40.

Defeat in the West and Dunkirk

The 'phoney' war ended abruptly on 8 April 1940 with the German invasions of Denmark and Norway, followed on 10 May 1940 by the invasions of France and the Low Countries. Those late spring and early summer weeks of 1940 have a nightmarish quality about them. Denmark and Luxemburg were overrun within hours, Holland and Belgium within days and France and Norway within weeks. The last British and Allied troops were evacuated from Dunkirk and, incidentally, from Norway on 4 June and France surrendered on 22 June. Britain was alone and beleaguered.

The evacuation of 330,000 troops (220,000 of them British) from Dunkirk and nearby beaches is writ large in the annals of the Second World War. The flotilla of 700 small ships (100 of which were lost) which assisted the Royal Navy has passed into legend and the evacuation – in reality the culmination of a massive military defeat – was widely regarded as a victory.

The diarist A.K. Goodlet saw it differently, and he was also alarmed by the recently appointed Prime Minister Churchill's morale-boosting speech in the House on the afternoon of 4 June (this was the 'we'll fight on the beaches… we'll never surrender' speech). Mr Goodlet reacted as follows:

> …Churchill's speech in the Commons rather fills me with disquiet. He (Churchill) spoke frankly about the appalling loss in guns and equipment we had suffered and praised the miracle of the evacuation, but what I did not like was the suggestion that if large parts of the country were subjugated … the government would be carried on from Canada.

The diarist's entry for 30 June 1940 undoubtedly mirrored the feelings of millions of Britons, however, when he wrote: '…and so finishes another half year and God grant the picture is a better and more cheerful one for this country and the world when I make the final entry in the volume for 1940. God save Britain.'

THREE

AIR ATTACKS ON BRITAIN AND THE IMPACT ON EALING, ACTON AND SOUTHALL: 1940-45

The weeks following Dunkirk saw frantic preparations against invasion and the epic Battle of Britain, which was largely fought in the skies over London and south-east England. Finally, in the autumn of 1940, the Germans began the heavy night-bombing of London and most of the other major British cities in a campaign which lasted until May 1941. This campaign, the Blitz as it became known, killed 30,000 civilians, injured many thousands more and caused widespread devastation.

Hitler, having failed to defeat Britain by a combination of aerial and sea power, then turned eastwards and hurled his armies against the Soviet Union on 22 June 1941. Britain was no longer alone and, when the Japanese attacked Pearl Harbour in December 1941 and the United States entered the War, the balance swung in favour of the Allies and against the Axis powers.

The Battle of Britain and RAF Northolt

A second wave of evacuees in September 1940 from London occurred whilst one of the most decisive battles of the Second World War was still being fought over south-east England. This, the Battle of Britain, raged from July to October in the most glorious weather. Vapour trails against a blue sky became a regular feature of life in London and its suburbs in what became known as the 'Spitfire Summer.' The importance of the Royal Air Force airfields in South East England in the battle cannot be overestimated and they were the express target for most of the enemy bombing raids. Had they been knocked out, the battle could have been lost and the invasion of the country a distinct possibility. Amongst the most crucial of the airfields was RAF Northolt, adjoining the Ealing Borough boundary.

The year 2005 will be Northolt's ninetieth year of operation – the longest of any RAF station. Northolt has, in fact, played a vital role in the defence of London and the South East in two world wars and is also the last remaining RAF airfield to have seen service in the Battle of Britain.

From July to November 1940, the station was the home base of some ten RAF squadrons, including three redoubtable Polish ones, which were equipped with Hurricane fighters and later with Spitfires. Very little aerial combat took place over Ealing, Acton and Southall since, thankfully, their interceptions were often over the south coast and, invariably, well to the south of London. A recent book, *The Northolt Story*, confirms that Northolt escaped serious damage during the Battle of Britain and the subsequent Blitz. Up to March 1941, large numbers of bombs fell within a two-mile radius of the station but less than twenty hit the airfield and not all of them caused damage. The worst damage was caused by a single raider in October 1940. Northolt's comparative escape was probably due to three factors. Its location to the north-west of London, its very effective camouflage and the interception of potential attackers many miles from the home station. The presence of this important target on the Ealing boundary did pose a threat to the people of Northolt and Greenford but, mercifully, most of the bombs which missed their RAF Northolt target fell harmlessly in the wide-open spaces which then surrounded the airfield and not on the two communities. Greenford's luck, however, partially ran out in the early afternoon of Monday 30 September 1940. The RAF diary described it thus:

Greenford area: A dive bombing attack was made by six aircraft at 13.50 hours when 100 bombs (HE) were dropped causing very severe damage which included 400 houses. A sub-station of the Uxbridge Electric Supply Co. received a direct hit and there was extensive damage to mains which affected 1,000 small consumers. The casualties so far reported amount to thirteen persons killed and 106 injured.

This preliminary report did not do justice to this Greenford raid – the damage and casualties were on a much greater scale. The grievous impact of this raid on the civilian population of Greenford will be described later.

The London Civil Defence Region (LCDR): 1940/41

From June 1940, the world's largest air force, the German air force, was within one hour's flight of the world's largest target, London. But the first German aims were the destruction of the Royal Air Force and its airfields in south-east England as a prelude to the invasion of this country. In this Battle of Britain – one of the decisive battles of the Second World War – the Germans suffered their first defeat of the war and, exasperated, began the heavy night-bombing of London in a determined effort to break the spirit of the people. The attacks were made almost entirely by three Luftwaffe aircraft types – the Heinkel (He III), Dornier 17 (Do 17) and Junkers 88 (Ju 88). All three aircraft, by RAF standards, were of medium size and range and, most importantly for the civilian population below, carried a modest bomb load. (The Germans, in fact, did not produce a really satisfactory heavy bomber aircraft during the Second World War.) With hindsight, the German bombing of Britain in the winter of 1940/41 seems insignificant when compared with the later bombing of Hamburg and Dresden, let alone of Hiroshima and Nagasaki. But the German raids were not insignificant. They were the first attempts in the history of warfare to subdue a people by mass aerial bombardment. Expert opinion in the 1930s was that no civilian population could endure bombing on such a scale but the British people proved the experts wrong – at great cost.

The first air raids on the LCDR began in August 1940 but the Blitz proper did not begin until the late afternoon of Saturday 7 September, when the Germans rained down high explosive and incendiary bombs on the docks and Thameside boroughs. They returned that night and for the following fifty-seven nights in what became, in effect, a siege of London. On 10 September the anti-aircraft defences were reinforced and a deafening barrage raised the spirits of Londoners. Its effect on the Germans was minimal – their losses averaged less than one aircraft a night and it was not until April and May 1941 that the defences began to take a heavy toll on the enemy. In late September and October the raids spread increasingly to west London and residents of our three boroughs began to feel the real impact of the bombing. The night of 14 October saw the beginning of very heavy raids and the casualty lists grew. On 14 November, London was spared when the Germans concentrated on Coventry and from then until the end of the campaign, raids on London were interspersed with attacks on other cities and towns. Sunday evening, 29 December 1940, saw

Dornier 17 (Do 17) bomber.

Heinkel (He 111) bomber.

Junkers 88 (Ju 88) bomber.

the devastating fire raid when the City of London burned in the second 'Great Fire of London'. The extensive damage caused by this raid led to compulsory 'fire watching' on all industrial, commercial and residential premises. There were more raids in the early months of 1941 and then in April came two very heavy and distinctive raids on the nights of the 16th and 19th. Some 700 German bombers took part on both occasions and damage and casualties were reported from most parts of the LCDR. Finally, on the night of Friday 10 May 1941, came the heaviest and last of the bombing raids of the 1940/41 campaign against London and the worst casualty figures. It was a cloudless night with bright moonlight and the Germans unleashed 700 tons of high explosive bombs and 7,000 canisters of incendiaries. 1,436 Londoners were killed and 1,792 were seriously injured; there were 2,000 fires and one third of the streets of London were impassable the next morning. Westminster Abbey, the Law Courts, the Royal Mint and the Tower of London were badly damaged and Churchill wept amongst the ruins of the House of Commons. Londoners were shaken but the Germans did not return in strength for many months – since most of the Luftwaffe was switched to the east in readiness for the German invasion of Russia in June 1941.

Ealing, Acton and Southall

The people of the three boroughs shared in the numerous air raids on London in 1940/41 and, as we shall see, suffered damage and casualties on many occasions during those dangerous nights. But the geographical location of the three boroughs was an advantage. Most of the German bomber squadrons approached the LCDR from the east and the south, and the eastern and southern areas of the region, together with the central London boroughs, endured the heaviest bombing and suffered the largest numbers of casualties. Let us look now at how the three boroughs fared in 1940/41 but, before we do, I would like to make a few observations on the terminology and contents of wartime reports.

First, researchers of wartime reports are struck by the widespread use of the word 'incident'. It is a bland, all-embracing word and so was ideal for those years of rigid censorship. A dud incendiary bomb falling into a duck pond was an 'incident', as was a V2 rocket falling on a crowded Woolworth's store, killing 160 people and injuring 200 more. I will try and use the word as little as possible in the details that follow.

Secondly, there are many gaps in local records – on the number of bombs dropped, on the damage caused and, more importantly, on casualties caused by specific bombs. There are some records for Ealing and Acton but very few for Southall and, where they do exist, they are often incomplete and are sometimes inaccurate.

Ealing

It is widely believed that life in the Ealing area was peaceful enough before the heavy bombing of London began in September 1940 but the sirens had sounded over fifty times in the three boroughs and the local anti-aircraft guns at Brentham, Gunnersbury Park and Wormwood Scrubs had opened up on several occasions. The first air raid on Central London had been on the night of 24 August, and bombs fell on the capital on succeeding nights.

Extracts from the diaries of Erica Ford give a taste of life during this period. Miss Ford, a young woman of twenty in 1939, lived in comfortable circumstances with her family in Mount Avenue and then Park View Road (from March 1941). She regularly attended St Peter's Church and was responsible for church flowers. She wrote:

*Bomb damage to electrical outfitters J. & M.
Stone, Ealing Broadway, September 1940.*

*Bomb damage in Mount Park Road, Ealing,
September 1940.*

Friday 23 August (1940). Four planes down. Early morning siren. We were awakened at 3.00 a.m. by gunfire and later the drone of an unfamiliar engine, most certainly German. We sat on picnic chairs in the hall (of the flats) with eiderdowns over us and were trying to get to sleep when the 'All Clear' went at 4.00 a.m., so back to bed. It was a wonderful moonlit night.

Followed by 'Saturday 24 August. Fifty planes down today. Three sirens (air raid warnings). Nineteen of our own (planes) down but the crews of twelve saved.' Later, her game of tennis was interrupted by another warning but completed after the 'All Clear'. Then: 'Lovely evening. Had bath and heard drone of a Hun. Searchlights brilliant. Siren went (again) soon after. Sat in hall. This lasted from 11.20 p.m. to 1.20 a.m.'

Miss Ford later had to enrol for work of 'national importance' and worked shifts in the canteens of the National Fire Service. She weathered the change from an ordered and leisurely life to a markedly different and much tougher one very well – like so many other British women in the war years.

The frequent pre-Blitz warnings without bombs had bred a certain indifference, locally, but a rude awakening was to come with the first bombs on the district on the second night of the London Blitz.

In Ealing, the first bombs fell on the night of 8 September 1940 in and around Greenford Park cemetery, Argyle Road, and the Mount Park area. Bombs (high explosive and incendiary – sometimes unexploded) and anti-aircraft shells and shrapnel were reported on every night of September from the 8th onwards. Erica Ford's experience of the first enemy bombs was as follows:

Sunday 8 September. At 9.35 p.m. there was a terrific crash and it shook the place. M. and E. rang to say a delayed-action bomb had dropped in Mount Park Road and all the evacuated people were sent to St Peter's Church. Five people turned out of their homes came in and had a cup of tea with us. There were more awful crashes. We had a rotten night. One of the worst.

During September, Miss Ford made mention of bomb damage in Ellerton Road, the Ealing Common Station area, Argyle Road and the Pitshanger Lane area. She also referred regularly to the loud gunfire from the guns in nearby Brentham.

A note on the Anti-Aircraft (AA) defences of the capital would be timely at this point. With few AA gun successes and concerned at the state of civilian – and military – morale, the Commander-in-Chief of AA Command, General Sir Frederick Pile, called all his brigade and battery commanders in the London area to a conference in Central London on Tuesday 10 September. With London now being heavily pounded nightly, he stressed the urgent need to show the public that the defences could hit back. That night, he told them, as soon as the raiders arrived, every gun around the capital would shoot blindly into the night sky at a maximum rate of fire. The result was gratifying – civilian morale was boosted – but a cascade of shrapnel and, occasionally, unexploded AA shells fell on the London area, including our three boroughs. Enemy losses did not grow – they flew higher and a big toll of enemy aircraft was not achieved until near the end of the Blitz in May 1941. Youngsters like Roy Bartlett revelled in the row:

That night the racket was incredible. The guns in our local park (Gunnersbury) punched the ears like a heavyweight boxer and made the shelter floor tremble. Dad called me to the shelter entrance to hear the shrapnel pattering down like hail, and broken roof slates added to the racket.

Bomb damage in Westfield Road, September 1940.

The worst nights in the month for bombs and damage were the 19th, 25th, 26th, 27th, 28th, 29th and 30th. Four one-tonne parachute mines fell on Ealing during September. Five people were killed and two were injured when a mine demolished the Load of Hay public house at Greenford on the 24th, and six were killed and thirty injured on the following night when a mine caused widespread devastation in Medway Drive, Perivale. The King and Queen visited Perivale on the following day and inspected the damage. Two more mines fell on those nights without causing casualties, in the Ruislip Road playing fields on the 24th and on the GWR sports ground at Vallis Way on the 25th.

The Little Ealing School log paints a grim picture of those Blitz days and nights. After a second wave of evacuation, this time to Weston-super-Mare, the school roll in the summer of 1940 was 196 (105 boys and ninety-one girls). The log describes school life after the raids began in September 1940:

9 September: Following a night during which there was a nine hours raid warning and bombs were dropped at many places within the borough, only twenty-five children were present at 9.00 a.m. Latecomers brought the total to eighty-six.

13 September: An air raid warning was sounded at 9.45 a.m. – when 131 children were in attendance – and lasted until 2 p.m. The children and staff spent the 4½ hours in the trench (shelter) and protected cloakrooms. Biscuits and sweets were handed round at intervals and all concerned were in the best of spirits throughout the long wait.

The Load of Hay public house, Greenford, pre-September 1940.

The Load of Hay public house, Greenford, September 1940.

Left: *Bomb damage to Sanders' furniture store, Western Road, Ealing Broadway, September 1940.*

Below: *The King and Queen with the Mayor of Ealing, Perivale, September 1940.*

25 September: School did not open at all today owing to a delayed-action bomb having fallen in Weymouth Avenue. The staff reported to the Education Office and were allocated to various Ealing schools in the afternoon.

The log continues: '*30 September:* Owing to an oil bomb in the Infants' yard, the children from that department were accommodated in the Junior School this morning', and, later, notes that: 'Air raid warnings and gunfire disrupted school every day during September/October/November 1940 with a few calmer days.' The stress suffered by the children and, perhaps, even more so by the staff during these months of upheaval and danger can be imagined, and with it the damaging effect on the children's education.

During late September and October, the Luftwaffe tried to hit RAF Northolt airfield and, on one occasion, some 100 high explosive (HE) bombs straddled the area between Fermoy Road, Greenford and Eastcote Lane, Northolt. I have quoted from the RAF report on that bombing raid on the afternoon of Monday 30 September, but further investigations have revealed a much grimmer picture. The attack was carried out by six enemy aircraft at 13.50 hours on that day. The target was RAF Northolt, its hangars and surrounds. The small formation unleashed their bombs almost in unison – the only concentrated raid of this kind on the three boroughs. The aircraft would have carried 16 HE (50 kg) each with some canisters of incendiary bombs (IB) A fair proportion of the bombs would have failed to explode and others may have been delayed-action ('time' bombs). They fell well short of their target and straddled the residential area on either side of Ruislip Road, Greenford. The effect was grievous and, according to the post-war list of civilian war dead, thirty-seven people – men, women and children – were killed or fatally injured. Many more people were injured in varying degree. The dead were to be

Houses in Ruislip Close, Greenford, after a daylight raid, 30 September 1940.

Ruislip Road, on the corner of Eastmead Avenue, Greenford, after bombing in September 1940.

found in Avon Road, Beechwood Avenue, Braund Avenue, Creighton Road, Eastmead Avenue, Eastmead Parade, Glencairn Avenue, Glencairn Drive, Rosedene Avenue, Mornington Road and Verulam Road. The worst single incident was in Verulam Road where six members of one family were killed.

Two memoirs from Colin Emmins and Ray Lawlor describe the grim aftermath of the raid. Both men were very young children at the time of the raid and so quote mainly from their family recollections. Colin Emmins recalls:

On Sunday 30 September 1940 there was an unexpected daylight raid on Greenford. Bombs were dropped on Mornington Road (amongst other places, I dare say) and as the bomber flew off its rear gunner sprayed the street with machine gun fire. My cousin Beryl Peters, aged eight and with learning difficulties as they now say, was in the back garden of her home at no. 57 and although the fence fell on her she was otherwise unhurt. Her bright and active brother, my cousin Keith aged six, was not so lucky. A builder had left a heap of sand at the side of the road and, as little boys will, Keithie was playing with it. He was caught in the hail of bullets and killed.

Some houses were destroyed and others, like no. 57, were so badly damaged that they had to be pulled down, not before looters had picked over the contents. All this I remember only from family legend: I was five at the time.

After the war no. 57 Mornington Road was rebuilt. My uncle had always promised my aunt that they would never go back but in the event she did so and indeed remained there for the rest of her life, despite an unfulfilled dream of a bungalow at Shoreham-by-Sea.

Ray Lawlor also adds another sad chapter to that tragic day:

September 30th 1940 was a Monday although I wouldn't have known that at the time. I was at home with my mum as I was only four years of age and hadn't yet started school, but my two brothers and sister were at the Ravenor School which was a short distance away. I always knew it happened around lunchtime because of the knives and forks but I couldn't remember whether it was before or after lunch. I have recently seen the RAF diary for that day – it recorded events at 13:50, so it must have been after lunch. My sister confirms this because she and our brothers were making their way back to school having come home for lunch when the siren sounded. She says they hurried on to use the school's shelters rather than coming back home.

Everything went black. I have thought about this many times but have never been able to explain it satisfactorily. Was I knocked unconscious (I don't remember having a sore head afterwards); could it have been caused by a cloud of smoke and dust; or was it simply the shadow of a plane passing across the sun? When it was no longer black I remember I was standing in the dining room facing the French window into the back garden. My Mum was lying on the floor at my feet, facing upwards and there were knives and forks scattered across the floor. I called to her but she didn't answer.

Two ARP Wardens came along the alleyway at the bottom of the garden. They were dressed in black uniforms and wearing steel helmets – just like the ARP man in *Dad's Army*. They saw me crying and hopped over the back fence and came up the garden. The first one crouched down and took my right arm and I noticed it was bleeding. I said 'My Mummy', and the second man said he would check and went into the house through the French window, while the other bandaged my arm and hand. When the warden came out of the house nothing was said but I saw them exchange glances and, although I was only four, I knew.

I was taken to hospital – apparently it was St Bernard's in Southall which was being used as an emergency hospital. I remember being put into a bed and being left on my own and crying for my mum. I can remember crying for a long time. I have difficulty getting events in sequence from this point but I remember being carried into another building at night and seeing the outline of the apex against the sky. I recognised that building five years later – it was King Edward's Hospital in Mattock Lane, Ealing.

One of my brothers has since told me that I was discharged from hospital but had to return when my shrapnel wounds became septic. I don't remember this but my Discharge Certificate (12 December 1940) says I had septic shrapnel wounds, but I also remember a doctor using large shears to cut plaster from my arm and seeing dead skin hanging in shreds. I remember staying one or two nights with a lady – possibly an aunt, a few nights at St David's Home in Ealing where my Dad worked, and then a few weeks with some neighbours who had their Anderson Shelter erected in their lounge and I slept in there with their son of a similar age to myself.

I don't remember Christmas but sometime in February '41 my Dad took me to Abingdon where I met up with my brothers and sister who were living in a hostel after being evacuated on 5 October.

Every day, thousands of people made their weary way to work in Central London despite the vagaries of public transport in wartime. Amongst them was a lady from West Ealing who put down her reactions to life in the Blitz in letters to a close friend. These letters from 'Edith' appeared under the terse heading 'Wartime Letters' in a past Ealing publication, *Local Historian*. Edith's letters are graphic, highly informative and troubled, and reflect some of the torment and growing exhaustion felt by many during the Blitz months. In one of a series of letters to a 'Mr A', dated 24 September 1940, Edith wrote:

Last Wednesday, the 18th September, I was here at home and of course unable to even lie on the bed because Fritz was hovering overhead. Well, about 1.30 – 2.00 a.m. six whistles flew past this building, I counted them as I knew what to expect. They hit Northfields, killing man and woman in shelter and smashing down several houses and other people hurt. The explosion was terrific. Then the following day, Thursday, in the early hours of the morning, he hit and brought down completely three houses at the top of Lavington Road, you will know it, by the Drill Hall and St John's Church, to say nothing of bringing up the road. Also an incendiary bomb was dropped in Green's Stores in the main road opposite 'Rowses'. Police etc. did not think it was 'alive', in fact did not think it was serious, so it was <u>not</u> roped off. Out came the shoppers and at <u>10.30 a.m</u>., it exploded, killed several people and brought down part of the stores, the next three shops and houses to it. Brought up a crater in road. Traffic is <u>not</u> back along main road yet. Bomb dropped and set fire to those small houses by Deans Gardens and one on shelter. Same morning three bombs on 'Sanders' in Broadway, but lucky the fire girls AFS belonging to the firm sleep in shelter on premises. They tackled them and saved Sanders from fire. A small amount of goods were burnt. Christ Church got one and Bond Street was roped off for three days, a timed bomb fell there.

Last night bombs were dropped at Haven Green and Perivale and Brentham. Oh, Ealing Common last week was hit and shop windows smashed.

A complete street at Acton is down and in Hammersmith they do not know where they are not hit. Southall have had several smashes, I am hoping to post a *Gazette* to you this week, so you will read a little about it. I mentioned in my last letter about Oxford Street. It is pitiful. Selfridges are not open yet. They have a timed bomb on premises. All round Wimpole Street, Mandevill Street, in fact all that area is smashed. Edgware Road. I walked along in my lunch time today. The Scotch Wool Shop, Picture Place and Coopers Stores are smashed. It distresses me terribly to see the destruction and for what? Last night at 9.00 p.m. all the lights failed in London as far down as Acton. We managed with candles for about half an hour. Chelsea has suffered badly, and County Hall, am wondering how the National Liberal Club is standing all the shocks.

I came straight home as we have had two 'reds' this morning and a yellow as I left the office, so thought I was better in house. It is quite true what you read about people on the underground. Some of them settle down in the afternoon. Paddington Station every day is crowded with men, women and children going away.

I do not wonder you have not received any letters, you should see the mail bags waiting to be put on the trains.

I am expecting the siren any minute and you know it is on for the night. 'All Clear' at <u>5.45 a.m</u>. this morning. Started at 8 p.m.; at 4.30 a.m. this morning it was a racket. I had not even undressed to get to bed. There were seven of us, standing in a little corridor, and each one of us had to be on duty at 8 a.m.

What will be the end of it all? I can't believe we any of us can escape. Wasn't it cruel to sink the children's ship to Canada. I see several Southall children were on it.

The wireless does not give the name of the places hit. Paddington Goods shed, the glass was broken that came from the church that was hit, by Paddington. We are not allowed to pass Toll or Trunk calls at night all lines (Post Office) kept for emergency!

I am afraid I am writing very disjointed, but I am giving you just a small outline of damage. You see traffic is at present out of hand. You can only travel so far by train, then bus so far,

Bomb damage at St Benedict's church, Ealing, October 1940.

then train again if you want to go to the City. Don't feel very brave now. Everybody dreads the nights. Hours and hours I sit in my little hall praying for us all. No-one can do anything about it.'

Edith came through the storm.

October, like September, saw repeated bombing of the borough and bombs fell on no fewer than twenty-five nights – the four worst nights were the 1st, 10th, 14th and 20th. Amongst the buildings hit by bombs in October was Ealing Abbey (then Priory). Two high explosive bombs devastated the east end of the church; hasty repairs were effected and four bays of the church were brought back into use with the bombed section separated by a wooden screen. The Priory remained in this condition until 1962. There were eighteen nights of enemy activity in November with the 16th and 29th rated the worst. On the 16th a parachute mine exploded in mid-air over Boileau Road but caused no casualties. St Saviour's Church was also hit on the 16th and the interior of the church was gutted by incendiary bombs.

December saw eight nights of raiding with the worst raid being on the 8th. The incidents on that night included a parachute mine on Broughton Road, West Ealing, which caused heavy damage, killed fourteen people and injured seventy-five more. A second mine fell on

The Broadway, near the Green Man Hotel, October 1940.

Bomb damage at the rear of Leyborne Avenue, West Ealing, October 1940.

Bomb damage to houses on the corner of Humes Avenue and Boston Road, Hanwell, October 1940.

Endsleigh Road, West Ealing, but, fortunately, did not explode. The last four months of 1940 had seen seventy-three nights of bombing.

Heavy raids on provincial cities, coupled with bad flying weather, reduced the number of raids in the early months of 1941. They were restricted to seven nights in January, two in February and three in March. Similarly, there were only two nights of raiding in April but ten people were reported killed in Ealing on one of the nights and, finally, more bombs were reported on the night of 10 May 1941 – the night of the heaviest air raid of the war on London.

By the end of the 1940/41 blitz, over 600 high explosive bombs, several thousand incendiary bombs and six parachute mines had fallen on Ealing. They had caused heavy damage – particularly to residential property – and had caused grievous casualties. 190 citizens of Ealing had been killed, 269 had been seriously injured and 442 more had been slightly injured. And Ealing's ordeal was not yet over.

Acton

During the blitz of 1940/41, Acton suffered more, proportionately, than Ealing and much more than Southall. 330 high explosive bombs, several parachute mines and thousands of incendiaries fell on the borough. Few nights in September, October and November 1940 were free of

Above: *Bomb damage in Boston Road, Hanwell, October 1940.*

Right: *Bomb damage to the Playhouse cinema, Greenford, October 1940.*

Opposite: *Bomb damage to houses in Townholme Crescent, Hanwell, October 1940.*

incidents but the worst nights in terms of damage and casualties would seem to have been as follows:

September

20th: Church Path and Kent Road areas, and Rothschild, Bridgeman and Beaumont Roads; 25th: Perryn and Victoria Roads, Friars Place Lane and Midland Terrace; 28th: Alwyn Gardens and Horn Lane; 29th: a particularly bad night, including Springfield Court, Lynton Road, Chatsworth Gardens, Lexden and Grafton Roads and Horn Lane; 30th: The Link, Howard Close and Horn Lane, once again.

October

4th: a daylight raid hit Bollo Bridge Road; 8th: Gladstone and Beaconsfield Road. The Wesley Factory was hit by three HE bombs and suffered serious damage; 10th: Stephenson Street, Valetta and Old Oak Roads and First and Second Avenues; 12th: Hereford Road and Horn Lane; 13th: The Vale; 14th: Shaa Road; 16th: Carlisle Avenue and Hoylake Road; 25th: a second daylight raid on the borough resulted in industrial damage at Park Royal and elsewhere; 28th: Heathfield Road.

November

6th: Perryn Road and The Vale; 10th: Hoylake Road and Carlisle Avenue; 12th: a bad night, especially in the Horn Lane area, Princes Gardens, Norman Way and Osborne Villas; 20th: heavy destruction and damage at Blandford and Fielding Roads and The Avenue, 29th: again at Fielding Avenue.

St Saviour's church, The Grove, Ealing, November 1940.

December
11th: Mayfield Road and Lynton Road.

So widespread was the bombing in Acton that very few roads and streets in the borough escaped damage.

1941 saw far fewer incidents in Acton. A day raider on 28 January only succeeded in bombing open spaces but six people were killed in four other incidents and two unexploded mines had to be removed from the Great Western Railway and Western Avenue. As in Ealing, the Blitz had resulted in heavy damage to property and the casualty list for Acton for 1940/41 was ninety people killed, 130 seriously injured and a further 274 slightly injured. The 'baby blitz' of 1944 would add greatly to the list, however.

Southall

Southall shared fully in the dangers of the Blitz nights of 1940/41 but, when one considers its industrial importance, was perhaps more fortunate than Acton and Ealing in terms of damage and casualties. The most serious recorded incidents (and there is a paucity of records) were as follows. On the night of the 28 September 1940, the North Road School was badly damaged and was closed for six weeks. Then on the night of 15 October came another school incident. A bomb fell on the outside shelter at Tudor Road School but there were no reported casualties.

Ealing golf clubhouse, c. 1939.

Ealing golf clubhouse after bombing, November 1940.

Rear of Hartington Road, West Ealing, December 1940.

Salvaging at Jones & Knights, West Ealing, December 1940.

Acton Green bomb damage, September 1940.

Blast damage to the school, however, closed it for six months. Bombs fell near the Hanwell Viaduct, on the Uxbridge Road near the A.E.C. factory and on the boiler house of St Bernard's Hospital. 1940 saw bombs on Cambridge Road and South Road and in the High Street where Woolworth's store and a number of other shops were destroyed; it was widely felt at the time that the large gasometer in Southall acted as a guide to the bombers. The Hanwell Viaduct, a vital target, which was guarded against saboteurs, suffered near misses from bombs which fell on the golf links and on Uxbridge Road. Two allied aircraft also crashed near the viaduct.

Southall also suffered several daylight raids. In one of them, a German aircraft machine-gunned the town and, in another, damage was reported from Lady Margaret Road.

Two residents recall the aftermath of the bombs which fell on the Cambridge Road area of Southall in November 1940; Mrs M. Heath, who can never forget the incident when both her parents were killed when a bomb struck no. 6 Cambridge Road, and Keith Sorrell, who, after visiting a friend in Lady Margaret Road, returned to his parents' home in Cambridge Road at about 9.15 p.m. 'to find the house partly demolished and the rescue workers trying to release my parents from the wreckage. Alas, they were both dead.'

During 1940/41, 126 high explosive and hundreds of incendiary bombs fell on Southall and there was serious damage to commercial premises, schools and houses. Nineteen civilians were killed, sixty-four were seriously injured and a further eighty-two were slightly injured.

Bomb damage in Bridgeman Road, Acton Green, September 1940.

Bomb damage in Kent Road, looking towards Church Path, Acton, September 1940.

Firefighters in Hessel Road, 1941.

1942/43: The national scene

Most of the Luftwaffe bomber squadrons were moved to the Russian front in the summer of 1941 but squadrons in the west were occasionally reinforced to carry out reprisal raids on England.

1943 was the year of final victory in North Africa and at Stalingrad and was the turning point of the war. RAF, RCAF (Canadian) and USAAF air raids on Germany intensified whilst British home defences were greatly strengthened by new forms of airborne and ground radar. Once again, Hitler ordered reprisal raids on Britain and a number of sharp attacks were made on London. The year ended with the Luftwaffe at its lowest ebb but with the Germans planning revenge against Britain with new aircraft types and with 'secret weapons'.

The London Civil Defence Region

1942 was the quietest year for the London region since 1939. A few raiders penetrated to the outer suburbs but the worst incident occurred on 6 June, when a bomb which had lain undetected for thirteen months exploded in a Southwark street. The Germans carried out more ambitious raids on the region in 1943 and, on the night of 17 January, inflicted considerable damage and casualties.

Ealing, Acton and Southall

1942 was a quiet year in the three boroughs and no serious incidents or casualties were reported. One unexploded bomb was discovered in Ealing on 4 February and was rendered harmless.

Bomb damage in Templeman Road, Hanwell, June 1943.

A policeman surveys the bomb damage in Templeman Road, Hanwell, June 1943.

In 1943, the increased enemy activity against the London region was reflected in reports from Ealing and Acton. A number of unexploded anti-aircraft shells were dealt with in Ealing in January but the first serious incident of the year was in Acton on the night of 19 May at the junction of Park Road North with Park Road East. Four people were reported killed in Acton with others injured. Only two bombs fell on Ealing in 1943 but one on the night of 15 June caused damage to residences and killed seven people with a further eleven seriously injured in Templeman Road, Hanwell.

There are no reports from Southall on bombing in 1942 and 1943.

1944/45: The national scene

Enemy air activity against Britain increased greatly in 1944. The early months saw a resumption of heavy raids on London – most of them failures – as were heavy raids aimed at Hull and Bristol. It was a measure of the decline of the once mighty Luftwaffe but also a reflection of the highly effective British anti-aircraft defences. June 1944 saw D-Day and the successful Allied invasion of Europe and the launching of the first German secret weapon, the V1 flying bomb, a third wave of evacuees from London (after 1939 and 1940) and, from September onwards, the V2 rocket. Both weapons were aimed principally at Greater London with V1 forays against Southampton and northern England.

1945 was the year of victory – over the Germans in May and over the Japanese in August. Before the surrenders, massive allied air raids had been made on both countries. The two atom bombs dropped on Hiroshima and Nagasaki in August 1945 hastened the Japanese surrender and ushered in the nuclear age.

On the Home Front, the Germans continued their V2 rocket attacks on the London region, reinforced in March 1945 by occasional V1 flying bombs launched from western Holland. The few piloted bombing raids of 1945 were restricted to attacks on bomber airfields in Yorkshire, Lincolnshire and East Anglia. The last enemy missile to fall on Britain in the war was a V1 flying bomb which fell at Datchworth, Hertfordshire, on 29 March 1945.

The London Civil Defence Region

In January, February, March and April of 1944, the Germans resumed their air raids on the London region in a series of attacks which became known as the 'baby blitz'. The heaviest raids were on the nights of the 18th, 20th, 22nd and 24th February and the 14th March. Heavy calibre bombs (including 2,500kg high explosives and larger incendiary canisters) were used and the bombing caused extensive damage – including parts of west London. The raid on the night of 18 April 1944 was the last raid by manned aircraft on London.

The first V1 flying bomb (of which more later) fell on the night of 13 June but the main attack did not begin until 15 June and continued until 1 September. By that time, the air and ground defences had got the measure of the flying bombs. The attack was continued by air-launched bombs until January 1945 and then, finally, by more ground-launched V1s from western Holland in March 1945.

The first V2 rocket landed in Chiswick on 8 September 1944 and the attack continued, with one small break, until 27 March 1945. January and February 1945 were the worst months of the attack. Some notes on the V weapons follow.

The V1

The V1 (Vergeltungswaffe Eins – Revenge Weapon No.1) was known variously as the pilot-less plane, flying bomb, buzz-bomb or doodlebug, and was a remarkable weapon. It was cheap to produce; could reach a maximum speed of 400mph at a height of 2-3000ft; carried about 1 tonne of explosive with twice the blast effect of TNT and could be launched from ground ramps or from aircraft.

The V2

With the advent of the V2 rocket, warfare entered a new dimension. The rocket was 46ft in height; weighed 12 tons; had a 1 tonne warhead (similar to the V1); had a range of 200 miles which it covered in four minutes; travelled through the stratosphere with the speed of a bullet, reached a height of 55-60 miles and was launched against London from mobile trailers in western Holland. The only defence against it was to attack the launching sites (but they were mobile) or, more profitably, the supply lines and storage depots. The first V2 landed in Staveley Road, Chiswick, at 6.53 p.m. on 8 September, killing three people and injuring seventeen more and the last one fell at Orpington on 27 March 1945.

The robotic nature of the V weapons held a particular horror for people. One local lady spoke for many when she said that she preferred the piloted bombers of the Blitz year – since they, at least, had the 'human touch'.

Ealing, Acton and Southall

On 21 January 1944 the first of a new series of heavy raids (the 'baby blitz') began, and from then until the end of March London had thirteen major attacks which, after a long lull, proved very dispiriting for the citizens of the capital. The Germans used bigger, more destructive bombs and with the new rocket gun batteries below created an unprecedented din. The attacks were short, sharp and concentrated, and, on several occasions, swept into London from the North West – a tactic which greatly increased the threat to the war-weary people of Ealing, Acton and Southall. *The Gazette* newspaper printed a letter in 2004 from James Darbon, then of Acton, on the sixtieth anniversary of the 'baby blitz' in which Mr Darbon wrote:

> I had just celebrated my ninth birthday and it became another of my childhood memories… The climactic event for Acton came on February 24th. I was in my grandparents' home in Park Road North when a bomb seemed to be coming straight for us. Everyone was frantically looking for a corner to find safety. Fortunately, it veered away but landed less than a hundred yards away between Palmerston Road and All Saints Road. Nine houses were shattered. Later, when we returned home to Fletcher Road we found that the house of a friend had received a direct hit. The scene was one of utter devastation. Seven houses had been demolished and twenty friends and neighbours killed. Many other houses, including our own, were damaged. A similar scene was being repeated in other places such as St Albans Avenue, Bayham Road, Somerset Road, Carlton Road and the Speldhurst Road area…. When today's children are taught of the liberation of Europe they should also be told of those who were in the front line, where they, nowadays, live in peace.

Mr Darbon is surely right.

In Acton, which suffered severely, the worst nights were those of the 20th, 22nd, 23rd and 24th of February and of 14th March when large numbers of incendiaries, including phosphorus bombs, fell together with heavy calibre, high explosive bombs. Fifty-three people were killed in the February raids, including fourteen in Hale Gardens and a further twenty in Fletcher Road. There was extensive damage to housing and amongst the public buildings damaged were the Town Hall (by an AA shell) and the government building in Bromyard Avenue.

Bombs and a large number of anti-aircraft shells also fell on Ealing causing damage and casualties in Northcote Avenue in February 1944. No serious incidents are on record for Southall during these last piloted air raids on London. When the sirens sounded the 'All Clear' on the morning of 19 April, they signalled the end of the manned air raids on the area but, within a few weeks, flying bombs were being launched against the London area.

The V1 and V2 campaigns

Twenty-five V1 flying bombs fell on the three boroughs between June 1944 and March 1945 and a further dozen or so fell close enough to the boundaries to cause damage within the area

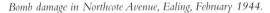

Bomb damage in Northcote Avenue, Ealing, February 1944.

High morale in Studland Road, Hanwell, 1944.

but the only V2 rocket incident occurred on 6 November 1944 when one of the missiles burst in mid-air over Ealing. Parts of the rocket fell in South Ealing and the heavier element fell in the Mount Park area. The arrival of the flying bombs in London and south-east England created a third wave of evacuation (the others were in September 1939 and September 1940) and, once again, thousands of school children, nursing mothers and other adults left Ealing, Acton and Southall for safer areas of the country.

As in the Blitz of 1940/41, Ealing Acton and Southall were more fortunate than districts to the east and south. The nearer you were to the V1 launching sites in the Pas de Calais and adjoining areas of France, the more you suffered. The V2 rocket figures also showed that East London, south-east London and Essex suffered most severely in that campaign.

The fall of the V1 flying bombs is best shown in calendar form, seen below.

V weapon attacks on Ealing, Acton and Southall: 1944

June
16th, Acton:
Wesley Playing Fields, North Acton Road – eighteen people seriously injured and sixty-eight more slightly injured.

18th, Ealing:
Whitton Avenue West, opposite Malden Avenue, Greenford – nine people seriously injured, four slightly injured.

19th, Southall:
(1) The first V1 fell close to Norwood Rectory in Tentelow Lane; seriously damaged the house which had to be demolished and caused a small number of casualties.
(2) Two hours later a V1 fell close to the boiler house of St Bernard's Hospital. No casualties reported.
(3) Three hours later, a V1 fell in the garden of no. 183 Tentelow Lane causing heavy damage in the vicinity. The damage and casualties caused by the two Tentelow Lane fly bombs were: six houses destroyed, two seriously damaged and 1,238 slightly damaged. One person was killed, one died later from her injuries and a further three were slightly injured. A bad day for Southall.

22nd, Acton:
East Acton Lane, near the Shepherd's Bush Cricket Club. East Acton Baptist Church was seriously damaged and there was damage to industrial premises. Four people were slightly injured.

23rd, Ealing:
Deans Road, between Montague Avenue and Cambridge Road, Hanwell. Extensive damage and twenty casualties, of which thirteen were fatal. This was Hanwell's worst single incident during the war.

23rd, Acton:
Fletcher Road, by Beaumont Road. The report referred to twenty houses being destroyed but did not specify casualties or damage caused.

26th, Acton:
This bomb fell during the lunch hour on Southfield Road, near Rugby Road. Twenty-five houses were destroyed and many others damaged in varying degrees. There were casualties but the number and type were not stipulated in the report.

27th, Acton:
V1 fell on no. 22 East Acton Lane and demolished seven houses. At least 800 more houses were damaged in varying degrees.

July
3rd, Ealing:
In the early hours of Monday morning, at the junction of the High Street and the Broadway. Heavy damage to John Sanders department store – the western end of which was demolished, as was the Railway Hotel. Widespread damage in central Ealing, including Christ Church. The early hour prevented heavier casualties. Five seriously injured, six slightly injured.

3rd, Southall:
A bomb on Southall Park caused widespread damage in central Southall. Buildings damaged included Holy Trinity Church (with its modern stained glass), the police station and a public house. Casualties were light. Four people were slightly injured. A bad incident occurred on Friday 7 July, in the afternoon when a bomb fell on the EMI factory at Hayes and a concrete

V1 bomb damage to John Sanders Ltd, Ealing, July 1944.

V1 bomb damage in Cuckoo Avenue, Hanwell, July 1944.

Opposite: *V1 bomb damage in Uxbridge Road, West Ealing, July 1944.*

roof fell on a number of people sheltering underneath. Casualties were the worst in this part of West London. Thirty-six killed, twenty-eight seriously injured and forty more slightly injured.

12th, Brentford:
A bomb near the Ealing boundary caused damage to Clayponds Hospital and to a day nursery. No serious casualties were reported

19th, Southall:
The Aviary in Windmill Lane. Slight damage and one person slightly injured.

20th, Ealing:
Cuckoo Avenue, near Kennedy Road, Hanwell. One killed, five seriously injured. No details of damage or of those people who were slightly injured.

20th, Acton:
Park Royal Road, near Serk Radiators on the Trading Estate. Heavy damage to factories. Three killed, twelve seriously injured and forty-two slightly injured. Another report, however, mentioned seven dead.

21st, Ealing:
The worst single incident in the three boroughs. Bomb on Uxbridge Road, West Ealing, between Hartington Road and Drayton Green Road. The explosion blocked Uxbridge Road,

V1 bomb damage, Uxbridge Road, July 1944.

destroyed five shops and caused heavy damage within a half-mile radius. Twenty-three people were killed, six were seriously injured and 148 were slightly injured – mainly shop workers and shoppers.

23rd, Southall:
West Middlesex Golf Course. No casualties reported.

31st, Ealing:
The Brent Valley Golf Course, between Church Road and Studland Road, Hanwell. No casualties. Damage was also reported on this day from a Wembley V1 to premises in Hanger Lane, north of Western Avenue.

August
20th, Ealing:
(1) Brookfield Road, between Ainsdale and Kingfield Roads. Ten houses reported destroyed with many others damaged. No reports of casualties.
(2) The second of three V1s fell at 10.30 a.m. on the Glaxo factory in Greenford Road. The Laboratory and Food Blending floor were destroyed and there was widespread blast damage. Seven NFS firemen were slightly injured.
(3) Meadvale Road, between Denison Road and Holyoake Walk. Forty houses destroyed or demolished, widespread residential damage. Five fatal casualties (including one Canadian serviceman), thirty-seven seriously injured and a further forty-eight slightly injured.

V1 bomb damage to Glaxo Co. laboratory, Greenford, August 1944.

V1 bomb damage, Meadvale Road, August 1944.

21st, Acton:

Churchfield Road East. Heavy damage. Five people killed and two missing, seven seriously and sixteen slightly injured.

24th, Ealing:

Ealing Road at the junction of Rowdell Road, Northolt. Eight seriously injured (including seven ATS girls) and thirty-three slightly injured (twenty ATS).

30th, Southall:

On this Tuesday afternoon, and within hours of the end of the worst stage of the V1 bombardment, Southall suffered its most destructive incident. The V1 fell on the Regina Road/ Adelaide Road area and caused widespread damage. Twenty-seven houses were destroyed, 132 were seriously damaged and 1,030 more were slightly damaged. One person was killed, thirty-four were seriously injured and a further forty slightly injured.

November

6th, Ealing:

The only V2 rocket incident in the three boroughs occurred on this day when a V2 burst in mid-air over central Ealing. Parts of it fell in South Ealing and the heavier element fell in the Mount Park area.

The worst V2 incident nearest to the three boroughs was at 10.00 p.m. on 14 February 1945. A rocket hit a block of flats on the Cleverley Estate, Shepherd's Bush, and destroyed the building. Twenty-nine people were killed, thirty-seven were seriously injured and fifty-nine more were slightly injured. A tragedy made worse by the fact that victory in Europe was only a few weeks away.

March 1945

14th, Ealing:

Greenford. The last incident in the three boroughs, and the last serious V1 incident of the war, occurred on this night. A V1 launched from Holland fell near the Ordnance Depot on Long Drive. Fourteen people were killed, eleven more were seriously injured and seventy-eight were slightly injured. Interestingly, this event was not recorded in the Ealing Civil Defence files.

Some more V1 facts

Evacuation of mothers with young children and of schoolchildren seems to have begun around the end of June 1944 and several thousands left the three boroughs. A glance at the local papers of the time shows, however, that life in the boroughs continued remarkably normally. Look-outs were posted on high buildings and factory roofs to give warning of imminent danger and the newspaper columns were filled with details of cricket matches (it took more than a war to stop those), summer concerts in the parks, baby shows and dancing in Springfield Gardens, Acton, and in Walpole Park, Ealing.

Some more facts and figures on the V1 damage and casualties:

Ealing: Fifty-three killed, seventy-three seriously injured and 382 slightly injured – a total of 513.
Acton: Thirty killed, eighty-four seriously injured and 272 slightly injured – a total of 386.
Southall: Three killed, forty-seven seriously injured and forty slightly injured – a total of 90.

There are specific figures for residential damage.

In Ealing, in addition to public and commercial buildings, seventy-seven houses were destroyed and 9,662 were damaged in various ways, in Acton seventy-one houses were destroyed and 4,848 were damaged and in Southall, thirty-three houses were demolished, 294 suffered serious damage and a further 3,124 were slightly damaged. In all, a thousand casualties plus dozens of houses destroyed and thousands more damaged, and with severe damage in the centres of Ealing and Southall.

Three personal recollections of life under the V1 attacks now follow – from Roy Bartlett, then aged fourteen years; from Jim Stockford, then aged eight years and living in Southall, and from Terry Fitzpatrick, then aged seventeen years and an army REME apprentice tradesman in Greenford.

Roy Bartlett left school in the summer of 1944 for his first job as a junior stores assistant in the AEC factory in Southall and in time for the V1 flying bomb offensive. He writes:

One Sunday morning the Bartlett family were pottering about doing their own thing. The sirens had sounded but life carried on. One advantage of the 'doodlebug' was that normally it could be heard approaching, then, if the engine stopped, there were about another twelve seconds before the blast.

We heard one coming close by and stood transfixed as it passed directly overhead. 'Please keep going' was the fervent, albeit selfish, wish. We sighed with relief as it droned on before cutting out. We counted down the seconds to the distant impact. We dashed up to the top of the house to see the now familiar plume of smoke a few miles away in the direction of Northolt. Next morning we heard that it had struck the Glaxo factory in Greenford. Thank God it was a Sunday. Had it been a normal working day there must have been heavy casualties among the workers.

And, on joining AEC and arriving at the stores:

I was shown the location of the air-raid shelter and it was explained that to avoid loss of production, work carried on after the siren sounded – relayed through the factory loudspeakers. Spotters on the roof then determined any immediate danger and would sound a howling klaxon. Basically this meant, run like hell!

The local warning systems were to be found in most large places of employment in the areas under attack.

Jim Stockford, then a young schoolboy in Southall, remembered in the columns of *The Gazette* in 2004, an incident which occurred locally on the afternoon of 30 August 1944. On that day a V1 flying bomb wrecked twenty-seven houses and damaged many more in Regina Road, Southall. Mr Stockford writes:

One woman was killed and several were seriously injured or trapped under wreckage. The local newspaper reported there would have been far more casualties had many residents not been out of their homes at the time. One family had a lucky escape. Their house was destroyed as they sheltered just a few feet away in their Anderson shelter in the garden. They lost their home but they emerged, shocked and frightened, but unharmed. The paper reported that the injured were pulled out of the wreckage by civil defence workers and American troops whilst a doctor administered morphine to one woman who was pinned down and badly injured. American troops meanwhile covered bombed roofs with tarpaulin to keep out the rain.

The last enemy blow on the three boroughs – with a terrible irony – managed to hit a military target. Terry Fitzpatrick, then a young soldier, had been posted to the Army Ordnance Depot in Long Drive, Greenford, in May 1944 and experienced a personal near miss on 14 March 1945 – a few weeks before the end of the war in Europe. In his article to the BBC WW2 website 'People's War' Mr Fitzpatrick writes:

As far as we were affected in Greenford, most doodlebugs petered out well before we got too concerned. The rescue services used to reckon they would drive out along Western Avenue to watch them until they cut out and then track their glide path to the final location.

But eventually our day came. Air raid drill was to cower down beneath the solid timber benches on which we worked to repair/maintain telecomm apparatus. When danger was not too close this sheltering was a not bad experience as I worked in a group with four ATS women! On the day of the hit we took cover and waited. This time it got serious. We heard the famous duff motorbike noise – and it cut out! The whistling noise – and then the loudest crashing bang and pressure shock. The roof of the workshop lifted bodily and fell back on its walls – shooting years of dust and debris throughout the place.

We seemed to get ourselves together and all stumbled out into the open air without much but scratches, choking and shock. Outside was chaos. It was a direct hit on the adjacent building – walls blown out and roof demolished. Casualties were limited to the unlucky four or five who worked in this store building (we would have suffered worse as there were some 40/50 in our workplace). We did have one fatality however and this was poor old Paddy, our workshop handyman who had been on his usual shortcut past the back of the flattened store shed with the morning tea trolley – not good.

The overall bombsite scene was quite surreal as the store had contained a large number of recoil springs for 25-pounder guns – each spring being some 200mm diameter and about 1.5m long. They had dispersed everywhere, probably bouncing away after the up-heaving. Perhaps the springs also saved us from some of the blast effects (one large spring lost its inertia in demolishing my bicycle).

We all left the depot to recuperate for the rest of the day. I guess I was pretty disturbed by the event as, later in the day, I remember finding myself in Holy Cross church – strange for a non-believer.

As for chance, luck or whatever, I often wonder how much side wind would have been needed to change the course of the V1 so that it landed just thirty metres to the north at the end of its 100-mile trajectory – to make the writing of these comments very unlikely!

Civilian casualties and material damage: 1939-45

The cost in civilian dead and injured, together with details of material destruction and damage in the three boroughs, are given below:

	Killed	Seriously Injured	Slightly Injured	Total Casualties
Ealing	304	353	929	1586
Acton	163	290	546	999
Southall	22	111	122	255
TOTAL	489	754	1597	2840

Note: A further report reveals that nineteen people were buried but were unidentified.

Bombs and V weapon attacks

	High Explosive	Unexploded. High Explosive	Incendiaries	Mines	Unexploded Mines	Oil Bombs	V1s	V2s
Ealing	698	46	000s	6	1	32	11	1
Acton	369	N/A	000s	'several'	2	21	7	-
Southall	126	N/A	00s		N/A	N/A	7	-
TOTAL	1193		000s			53	25	1

Note: Incendiaries were too numerous to count and included explosive and phosphorous bombs.
N/A = not available.

Damage

No complete record exists for Ealing but the number of properties affected runs into thousands. Amongst public buildings destroyed or seriously damaged were St Saviour's Church and The Grove on 16 November 1940; John Sanders store and the Railway Hotel (*see* V1 section); Princess Helena College; Ealing Film Studios; Ealing Abbey (the 'Priory' in October 1940) and many commercial buildings in central and West Ealing. The residential damage was great – 618 houses were destroyed and 21,141 damaged in varying degree.

Acton records show that 512 buildings of all kinds (including houses) were destroyed or demolished later and a further 6,882 were damaged in varying degree.

Southall figures are mainly restricted to V1 damage (*see* above) but a large number of public and commercial buildings also suffered.

The worst-hit districts

The grim distinction of being one of the worst-hit districts in the current London Borough of Ealing must go to that part of West Ealing centred on Uxbridge Road and Broughton Road. Two of the Germans' most destructive air weapons – a parachute mine in 1940 and a V1 flying bomb in 1944 – fell on this district; devastated the shopping centre and many houses and caused serious damage over a wide area. They also caused heavy casualties. A total of thirty-seven people were killed, twenty-two were seriously injured and a further 207 were slightly injured.

Then, matching West Ealing in the number of fatalities, comes the residential area extending on both sides of Ruislip Road in central Greenford. This was the area wrongly targeted in the daylight raid on 30 September 1940 when some 100 HE bombs were unleashed prematurely – causing widespread damage and killing thirty-seven people.

To West Ealing and Greenford must be added Fletcher Road and the adjoining area of Bedford Park in Acton. Heavy calibre bombs in the 'baby blitz' and two V1 flying bombs, all in 1944, caused severe residential damage, killed some forty people and injured many more.

FOUR

PERSONAL RECOLLECTIONS OF LIFE UNDER FIRE

As mentioned in the Introduction to this book, personal recollections can illuminate history. Anecdotes can, in fact, be a valuable source of historical truth. Accordingly, members of the Ealing Museum, Art and History Society (EMAHS), local newspaper readers and others through the offices of Mrs Hilary Potts were invited to recall their wartime memories. Several people did so, sometimes writing at great length. They told of their reactions to evacuation, life in the shelters, travel disrupted by bombing and of the bombing itself, and some of their recollections appear below.

Evacuation and the outbreak of war

Thousands of children and adults were evacuated from the three boroughs in 1939, 1940 and 1944 officially and unofficially – and memories of those days live on.

From Mrs Alma Mansell:

I went to a village outside High Wycombe and managed to rent a farm cottage for my mother and aunt. One room down and two up; one water tap and a lavatory at the top of the garden. After about two years there, my mother brought herself back. She had a heart attack during a bad air raid and died a few days later. The funeral was delayed for a few days as it was difficult to get grave diggers.

From Mrs E. Mason:

We were very fortunate as we were very well treated and had excellent (evacuation) billets in Kingsbridge, South Devon. My friend and I were both attending Acton Central School but, somehow, after departing from Acton GWR station, the girls were left on Kingsbridge station but our boys were left in Dartmouth. Consequently our teachers had, among other problems, to commute to and from both towns when teaching their subjects. Going to Devon was my first experience of travelling so far by train (I was nearly fourteen). I returned to Acton in July 1940 in time to experience the Blitz.

Ironically, the majority of evacuees did the same thing, although some were evacuated a second time in 1940.
Nancy Nicholson, privately evacuated to relatives near Hatfield in Hertfordshire, recalls what became known as the 'phoney war':

There was a glorious St Martin's summer in September and October of 1939, contrasting grotesquely with the bad news from Poland, as city after city fell to the invaders… I wandered around the back lanes gathering berries, and had more fun with my girl cousins than the unhappiness of nations perhaps justified. I did go home (to Ealing) after Christmas (1939).

Miss Nicholson and her mother walking in North Ealing, after the fall of France (June 1940), reached Queen's Walk: 'All along the low gardens walls sat European refugees of various nationalities. Where were they all housed, I wondered.'

Tony Cozens was one of the children evacuated from West Acton Infants School in Noel Road to Holberton in Devon. Mr Cozens organized a reunion of evacuees in 1989 – fifty years on – and more than twenty ex-pupils attended. Mr Cozens reported that, 'there were quite a few people with tears in their eyes and it was all very emotional. We had a wonderful time down in Holberton'.
The party donated a plaque to the village.

The declaration of war on Sunday 3 September 1939 is recalled by William Burtt, then fourteen years of age, living at the time in Old Oak Common Lane, Acton:

Just before 11 a.m. the wireless was turned on. My first thought was that Mr Chamberlain seemed a very polite man. Why wasn't he calling Hitler all the names he could lay his tongue to? The old man was the first to speak: 'Here we go again!' he said. Later, the young Burtt set off for a walk with his dog. 'I got half way along Old Oak Common Lane, Bonnie trotting along happily beside me, when there was a distant wailing which became louder and louder. I realised it was an air-raid warning. I made it back to the house in two minutes flat. The family huddled in the air shelter until the sound of the 'All Clear'.'

Travelling in wartime

An EMAHS member remembers journeys to work from West Ealing station to Paddington during the height of the Blitz. The train services were irregular and there were times when up to thirty-five people were crammed into a compartment which normally held ten or twelve. Mrs Alma Mansell, who also travelled to Paddington with her brother (Mrs Mansell worked in a First Aid Post at the station), recalled that: 'If there was bomb damage on the track from bombing, bicycles were a necessity. Sometimes, with the odd hours I worked, I had to make my way by cycle during the air raids.' Bicycles were invaluable during the war years and getting to work, despite the hazards, became a matter of pride for many people.

Life under fire

In the air-raid shelters

Jane Harding remembers those dangerous nights clearly:

I remember nights of sheltering under a table when the sirens sounded and enemy planes were targeting the Acton area. One night an unexploded bomb fell next door to us at no. 2 Lynton Road and we had to leave our house in the early hours and walk to the special reception centre in the Congregational Church Hall in Churchfield Road, Acton – about a mile away. As a teenager, I found it all very exhilarating – with the crash of anti-aircraft guns and with searchlights illuminating the scene and making vivid patterns in the sky. We sat up all night, drinking cups of tea, and were allowed home in the morning ... it was my first experience of a night without sleep.

And from May Jeffries, also in Acton:

I spent many nights with my mother, brothers and sisters in one of the many shelters at the back of what was then called The Pensions Office in Bromyard Avenue, Acton. As there were so many of us, we were allocated a shelter to ourselves. We used to dread moonlit nights as we knew the enemy had a clear view of everything when air raids took place. We were unable to wear night clothes as space was too confined and we had to make do with sleeping on bunks in our everyday wear.

When the bombs fell

Jane Harding has recorded the memories of her neighbour, Joe Sullivan, of the bombing of his part of West Ealing:

The first air-raid damage was in December 1940, when a parachute mine fell on the gardens of houses on the west side of Broughton Road. Six houses in Broughton Road and nos 14, 16, 18 and 20 in Hartington Road were destroyed. At no. 18 a mother and father were in their shelter and survived, whilst their daughter, who had stayed in bed, was killed. Mr Sullivan's house, no. 17, had its roof blown off, windows shattered and the front door blown upstairs to the first floor landing. Mr Sullivan managed to rescue a lady from no. 14 through a hole in the flank wall. The Sullivan family, with seven children, were moved to Ashbourne Road, Hanger Hill, where they stayed till 1946. A block of flats now stands on the site of the demolished houses.

Even the dead were not left in peace, as the following extracts from the minutes of the Ealing and Old Brentford Burial Board, found by Mr B.J. Higgins, show:

Clerk reported that on the afternoon of 14 October (1940), during an aerial combat over the cemetery, an enemy plane dropped two bombs, which failed to explode, in the New Cemetery annex. ARP advised that one bomb should be covered in and forgotten (!), the one on the path should be roped off and removed. Temporary employee killed when house received direct hit. Next of kin have received full wages – receipt has been attached to wages book. Letter (January 1942) asking if the Board had any objection to the following inscription being put on a memorial, 'Murdered by German airman, Adolph Koch, on the night of 16th April 1941, Lest We Forget'... resolved that the inscription be allowed except that the name of Adolph Koch should be deleted.

Barbara Noble recalls the grim night in Northcote Avenue, Ealing, in February 1944:
It was a very noisy night with bombs falling. Just before 1.00 a.m. (on the 19th) I went into my mother's room at the rear of the house when the bomb fell. All the windows in the flat blew in – the glass from my window was all over my bed. I went outside looking for an old lady in the house next to the one hit ... helped her downstairs and took her back to our flat. Gradually I collected more people and others drifted in for warmth and companionship ... at intervals we

heard rumours of casualties, most of them fatal. I believe the final death toll was eight. I knew nearly every one of them, from my weekly stint of selling saving stamps.

From Mr C. Smith on the bombing of Southall:

My father was an auxiliary fireman during the war. The Germans dropped incendiary bombs and my father's division was called out. The bombs ... landed in the park, on Woolworth's in the Broadway, and at Lancaster Road. My father was up a ladder at the Woolworth's fire when part of the building collapsed. He had to hold on tight to the window frames, sustaining badly cut hands and bruising and was overcome by heat and smoke.

In 1944 came the V1 (flying bomb) campaign against London. Joe Sullivan remembers the single, worst V1 incident in the three boroughs:

On Friday 21 July 1944, a flying bomb fell on the Uxbridge Road between Hartington Road and Drayton Green Road, destroying Abernethie's shop and killing seventeen people (the final casualty figures were twenty-three killed and 154 injured). Among those killed was Mr Abernethie, who had come to pay his staff. Bodies were said to have been laid out on what is now part of the garden of no. 13 Hartington Road and false teeth have been discovered by gardening residents. The Post Office was damaged, as were Folletts, the garden shop, Humphreys, the hardware shop, Jones and Knight's and many other buildings.

Nancy Nicholson recalls the spectacular damage done by the V1 at the junction of the High Street and the Broadway, Ealing, as seen by her father:

He passed the bomb site where part of John Sanders, part of Sainsbury's, and the whole of Lilley & Skinner's and the Railway Tavern had been destroyed. The mannequins from Sanders' display windows had been blown into the road and policemen were patrolling to see that no looting occurred – not that anyone seemed inclined to loot. In those days, people were so generally honest.

And from Mr C. Smith, then a schoolboy in Southall:

I attended Featherstone School during the war and one day in the last year of the war (30 August 1944) one flying bomb came down in Regina Road, Southall, demolishing several houses and killing some people (official casualty figures – one person killed, seventy-four injured). Together with other pupils and school teachers, I was in lessons in a part of the school designated as a shelter. Suddenly the teacher motioned us all to lie down flat ... the blast broke several windows and brought the ceiling of the school hall down. Half an hour earlier, the headmaster had been taking assembly there.

Eileen Jameson, then a Southall teacher, has described classroom routine when the sirens sounded. The teacher had to collect the class register; ensure that all had left the room and then check the class numbers in the shelter. Teachers and children kept books for use in the shelter – each child had a jotter, an arithmetic book, a reader and a pencil. On days of frequent alerts, the children responded magnificently. They were quiet, orderly and knew the air-raid drill perfectly. But following the long, night raids, and with teachers often on fire-watching duties, the schools were often filled with tired children and tired teachers.

A daylight raid, aimed at Northolt airfield, brought destruction to the Greenford/Northolt area, and this graphic memory from Mrs Morland:

My best recollection of the war is of the manner in which the children were disciplined by the school staff in a heavy raid in September (1940). After passing through the bombed area to collect my child, I found the children sitting cross-legged in the school hall singing, 'She'll be coming round the mountain, when she comes' – totally unaffected by their ordeal. Their school (Ravenor) was in the centre of the bombed area and I was told that one bomb had fallen only six feet from their shelter.

John Chudley, born in 1936, spent the war years in the family home in Windermere Road, Ealing, and, because of his tender years, remembers the war years as being 'unremarkable'. His memories are remarkable, however:

We were provided with a 'Morrison' shelter, a heavy steel table affair with sharp, rough-cut edges which could be frighteningly dangerous if they came in contact with naked flesh. It was in the kitchen, the room in which we spent most of our time – reading, listening to the wireless, eating, etc. Beneath the metal table there was room for a small bed which I remember using during the days of the bombing. During air raids I would sometimes be joined under the shelter top by my grandmother. The anti-aircraft guns which were situated in Gunnersbury Park, about a mile away, would make a fearful noise and I can clearly see my grandma as she jumped in fright at every salvo. We would wait with bated breath as we heard the familiar whistling sound of falling bombs, followed by the explosions which came as a relief, and we selfishly gave thanks for someone else's tragedy.

One of the changes brought about by the Second World War was in the lifestyle of women who were required to take up employment. My grandmother, my aunt and my mother all began working at the King Edward Memorial Hospital in Mattock Lane, Ealing. Gran worked in the canteen as a cook, my aunt and my mother as clerical officers. It was while she was on duty in the hospital tower that a flying bomb flew past her and buried itself in Abernethies department store in the Uxbridge Road only two hundred yards away. I can remember her telling how she watched as the many dead and injured were ferried into the hospital by whatever means available.

This was the occasion of Ealing's worst flying bomb incident on Friday 21 July 1944, when twenty-three people were killed and 154 injured.

John Brett, twelve years old when the war ended in 1945, had a grim Blitz experience in Eccleston Road, West Ealing, where he lived with his mother, grandmother and two sisters. His father served in the war. He recalls:

An unforgettable experience happened to our family during the Blitz. The siren, situated outside our front door, had not sounded before an oil bomb hit our semi-detached house and at the same time hit a garage on the main road about a hundred yards away. An inferno resulted, during which time the dividing wall of our house collapsed, and it was only the quick action of my mother which saved my youngest sister who was lying on her bed. She pulled her away from the wall by her long dark hair. Unfortunately, the two elderly ladies next door who had the direct hit, had locked themselves into their bedroom, but had been quickly rescued by my father, on leave, and his friend. I remember that when the ladies appeared in the street their nightdresses were on fire. My mother tried to douse the flames with a blanket but I understand that they died on their way to hospital. As a result of this bombing we were allocated a 'requisition' house in Cleveland Road.

Eileen Eastham, whose local ties are with Southall, had two evacuation upheavals during the war, in 1939 and 1944. Her parents had moved to Southall from Blackburn in the early thirties when the cotton industry was hit hard. In 1939 they sent her, then aged six, to stay with relatives in Blackburn whilst they remained in Southall. They worked for the United Elastics Company which made khaki webbing etc. on round-the-clock shifts. Eileen was back in Southall within six months – in good time to experience the Blitz:

I remember the air-raid shelter at the bottom of our long garden path and my father in his uniform as an Air Raid Warden. The sirens would sound and off we would go down that path in the dark to our shelter. It was complete with kerosene lamps and camp beds. Great Aunt Alice lived in the flat above ours but she would never go to the shelter. She stood at her window saying the rosary through every raid. My father was once blown off the toilet by the force of a bomb which landed too close for comfort. It was always with a huge sigh of relief that we heard the sirens sound the 'all-clear' and we emerged from our shelters like rabbits out of burrows, not knowing what we would find or where the bombs had dropped – always thanking God that we had been spared.

I used to have a tin in which I kept the shrapnel that I picked up in our garden or on the way to school. During the Blitz we spent fifty-four days and nights in the shelters at school and at home. A landmine was dropped near our house and we were evacuated to a church hall until it was made safe.

We stuck it out in London until the doodlebugs (V1s) started and then my parents gave in and returned to Blackburn to live in relative peace. That was when I had to start wearing clogs and put up with being ridiculed for my cockney accent!

Marjorie Harris (née Cannon) was fifteen years old and living in East Acton when war was declared. With a younger brother and in the care of an aunt she was sent to Cornwall but, like so many evacuees, had returned to London by Christmas 1939. She became a shorthand-typist working in Oxford Street and, at nineteen, received papers calling for her to do factory work or nursing. She chose nursing. She remembers:

Early one Sunday morning I was woken up by a 'swooshing' noise and then a bang; it was a rocket (V2) which demolished a building in the grounds of the hospital. No lives were lost as the patients of that block had been evacuated the previous weekend. The explosion broke all the windows of the hospital but only a very few patients had been cut with glass. That day, we were allowed to wear a cardigan on duty!

At the hospital we ate quite well. We were issued with two jam jars each, one for a ration of sugar, the other for a little butter and margarine. On the breakfast table there was always a pot of Vitamin C tablets for us to take. We had blackout curtains and when the sirens sounded we had to pull all the beds away from the windows. This required a bit of strength and care.

We had very sad days when we heard of neighbours' sons missing or killed. We hated to see newspaper hoardings with the words saying that such and such a number of bombers had been sent on a raid and that only so many had returned.

Ken Chalk, then aged sixteen years and living in Park Avenue, Acton, was a member of the Home Guard – having 'upped' his age to get in. The incident he describes occurred near his home some two years after the end of the Blitz in 1941. He recalls:

I was awakened about 2.00 a.m. by, it seemed, somebody slamming a door shut very, very hard. I lay there for a few seconds and heard my father rushing down the stairs. I called out to him and he shouted for me to get up – a bomb had dropped.

Clothed, with his army greatcoat over his pyjamas, Ken Chalk emerged into the moonlit night. He continues:

When I arrived at the scene, there were lorries and wardens in attendance. It appeared that the pub and dairy at the junction of Park Road East and Park Road North had been blown up. I walked up the heap of debris where the pub had been and where the wardens were digging out an old lady who was waving her arm from below the debris. I helped the wardens as best I could and we got her out without too much trouble. As they laid her on a stretcher, one of the wardens, with the cardinal rule of the first-aider in mind, asked, 'Can I borrow your coat, soldier?' – the idea being that you didn't use your own! Of course, I gave it to him and away she went. I suddenly realised that I was standing there in army boots and pyjamas. I made my way home as quickly as I could, got back into bed and went to work next day like everybody else. Mum and Dad stayed up all night clearing up the glass where our windows had blown in. They also went to work the next day. I did manage to get my army greatcoat back – I would have had to pay for it if I hadn't.

There is a postscript to this story; Llewellyn's Dairy was owned by a lovely Welsh couple and both had been killed. Two more casualties of that war. I took my daughter and grandson back there some years ago – just grass now and a big block of flats. What ghosts must wander there…'

Mr Chalk's memory serves him well. The incident occurred on 19 May 1943 and the couple, Mr and Mrs Lewis, were both killed in Park Road North.

Dawn Binmore remembers an incident which involved her father, an engine driver on the Great Western Railway for many years:

During the Blitz he was on shunting duties at Acton Old Oak Common railway depot moving goods and wagons to their required positions. The air-raid warning sounded and he and his fireman dived off the engine and took cover under the neighbouring freight wagons. Bombs were dropping all around them for what felt like hours – though it probably wasn't. Eventually, the 'All Clear' went and they crawled out from their place of 'safety' to find that my father had selected a wagon on which was written 'EXPLOSIVES'.

Sidney Tibbles writes:

I was attached to the ARP Heavy Rescue Service in 1939. We were at a depot in Perivale that belonged to Ealing Council. Our time of duty was twelve hours a shift. One week on days and the other on night duty. I was a Heavy Rescue Driver, but most of the squad I was in were quite old men compared to me, so in the event of our rescuing people I had to do most of the tunnelling as I was the most active.

We had a fully qualified carpenter in the squad, so that when I was tunnelling he would shore up the brick rubble to prevent it from falling in on me. The story I'm about to write is one I cannot forget. It is and was so heartbreaking, although it was a long time ago. I am now eighty-three years of age, but I can still remember it well. I was on night duty when we were called out late at night because a bomb had hit a big house in Pitshanger Lane, Ealing, not far from the depot. It was a very cold night with the German bombers overhead, and with searchlights above and the Royal Artillery firing at them.

We got to this house, and I climbed on top of the rubble because the property had been completely destroyed. There I saw a man sitting upright, dressed only in a long white nightshirt, and I said to the carpenter, 'Here Len, here's one dead.' 'I'm not so bloody dead as you think I am,' the man suddenly said. 'Take these wooden beams off my legs and I'll be alright'. That we did and the first-aid people took him away.

Now I come to the heartbreaking part of the story. I then went to the bottom of the crater and there, with the aid of light from the torches that we had, I saw that all there was was a fireplace with a few embers burning, and lo and behold there was a woman sitting on a chair. She only had a nightdress on. It was cold and I rubbed her body for circulation. She was bleeding from a leg wound. Suddenly she said to me 'This is my fourth move. I came from Margate in Kent.' She then told me she had been breastfeeding a baby which was blown from her, and although she was conscious she was quite clearly delirious. However, we were concerned that there may well have been a baby, and so we looked around and suddenly we saw the baby with his head upside down on some rubble. I can still see its little legs kicking away.

I picked the baby up and gave it to its mother and suddenly she started crying, and so did I. It was all so sad. Suddenly she kissed me and said 'I have three more children somewhere. They were upstairs.' So myself and Len went to the top of the crater and part of the gable of the roof was laying on the ground. I crawled underneath it and found a gas stove, and also a bed which had apparently collapsed forward as a result of the floor caving in. I called out 'Is anybody there!' three times and then faintly I heard a voice say, 'Yes, and it's very cold.'

It was a very young girl who was very lucky because as the bed had rolled through the collapsed floor so the bedclothes went with her and she was saved, but unfortunately we were unable to find any trace of the other two children. Whether or not the day shift found any other persons alive I don't know, but I wouldn't imagine so.

The writer, Wm. J. Drinkwater, Southall born and bred, had volunteered for ARP duties (later Civil Defence) whilst awaiting his military call-up. Mr Drinkwater was assigned to Southall Casualty Services and, with a knowledge of first aid, was made a stretcher-party leader and given a distinguishing white helmet. By the spring of 1940, his section was fully equipped, proficient in their work and knew the first-aid manual from cover to cover, but they had still to be put to the test. The Blitz on London began on 7 September and soon afterwards the bombs began to fall on West London. Mr Drinkwater now takes up the story:

The raids generally began at dusk with a warning siren around six o'clock – just as the BBC News was starting on the radio. We immediately took to the shelters – people in their houses retreated to their Anderson shelters which could be found in nearly every back garden whilst we, in the casualty services, took cover in our sand-bagged hutment and prepared for action. Raids frequently lasted all night long, and the 'All Clear' sounded about seven o'clock in the morning. We would hear the crump of bombs as they fell, and wondered where they had dropped. It was not until we received the telephone information calling us to action that we knew the location. It was always an uneasy time wondering if our homes and families were affected.

Our baptism of fire came one dark night during the height of a raid. A stick of bombs had demolished shops and damaged cottages opposite. We were quickly on the scene but could do little before the rescue teams had checked and reported. In the meantime we searched the cottages for residents – finding them in the shelters or in cupboards under the stairs and consoling and reassuring them.

By this time, Mr Drinkwater and his colleagues had to work twenty-four-hour shifts (there were bunks in the hutments) and had every other day off but, even then, they were nearly always in a 'state of preparedness.' Mr Drinkwater continues:

I remember well the night when London was set on fire (on Sunday 29 December – this night became known as 'The Second Great Fire of London'– after which fire-watching duties became compulsory). We were some twelve miles away in our depot in Southall, but the glow was so bright that the whole surrounding countryside was lit up and it was almost like day. I recall, too, visiting the City afterwards and noticing that the gutters near the Docks were filled with metal which had flowed molten during the conflagration.

When daylight raids occurred we would be called away from meals to attend incidents. The sights were often pitiful to see. We helped in any way we could. The saddest situations were when children were involved. The strength of our services was continually being weakened by military call-ups and in due course I went for my medical examination at Hounslow Barracks. About this time, the government decreed that personnel on particular duties, like we were, would be exempted temporarily from military service.

And so it was for Mr Drinkwater until he returned home one day in early 1942 to find a familiar brown envelope waiting for him. It contained his call-up papers, a postal order and a travel voucher to Leicestershire – he was about to become a soldier.

A West London suburban lady who prefers anonymity wrote movingly in her diary, in mid-November 1940, that not all the members of a family could come to terms with the strain of week after week of enemy bombing. She wrote:

At about ten o'clock (p.m.) things began to hum and developed into quite the worst raid we've had yet, with a terrible noise barrage. We didn't attempt to go to bed until midnight; we were all very much on edge. My sister and I got into our bed and my brother went into his room – and he never came out again that night. But my father was unashamedly jittery – for the first time – and neither he nor my mother made any attempt to go to bed.

Finally there was a series of horrible whistles overhead, but no explosives. My father started to look for incendiaries (it turned out he was right) and went to the door about six times in his pyjamas. When things were a bit quieter he twice went down to his bed in the dining room; but each time the barrage immediately burst over again and he came trotting back. None of us slept until about 3.00 a.m. and even then I could still hear the guns thudding away through my sleep.

The milkman, as usual, that morning, called out: 'A wicked night.'

Sometimes, the distress of people whose 'nerve had gone' was compounded by the fact that they had appeared to be the most imperturbable. The unpleasant syndrome – of progressively worsening terror with each new experience of danger – could affect all kinds of people; old and young; male and female; soldier and civilian; but mercifully it affected only a small minority of the population who endured heavy bombing.

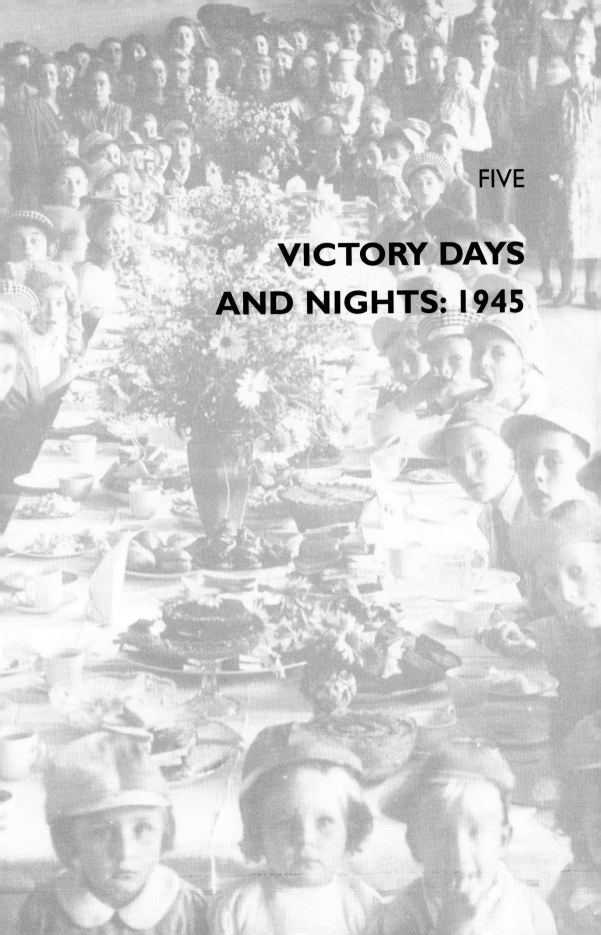

FIVE

VICTORY DAYS AND NIGHTS: 1945

Unlike the end of the First World War in 1918, which saw one tumultuous celebration, the ending of the Second World War was celebrated in two instalments – Victory in Europe (centred on VE Day, Tuesday 8 May 1945) and Victory over Japan (on VJ Day, Wednesday 15 August 1945).

VE Day

VE Day and the following days were filled with celebrations in the three boroughs and these events were fully recorded in the local newspapers; the *Middlesex County Times* and *West Middlesex Gazette* (for Ealing and Southall) and the *Acton Gazette* and *West London Post* (for Acton).

In Ealing, there were bonfires, thanksgiving services in all the churches, street parties by the hundred and flags and bunting in abundance. Hundreds danced on Ealing Green, two huge bonfires blazed on Horsenden Hill, and searchlights weaved a crazy pattern in the sky. Packing cases from Ealing Studios, park benches and deck chairs fuelled the bonfire in Walpole Park and an effigy of Hitler was burned in Greenford. On Sunday 13 May, contingents from the Armed Forces, Home Guard, Civil Defence and junior organisations paraded at a service of thanksgiving in Walpole Park. A similar assembly, attended by several thousand people, was held in Ravenor Park, Greenford.

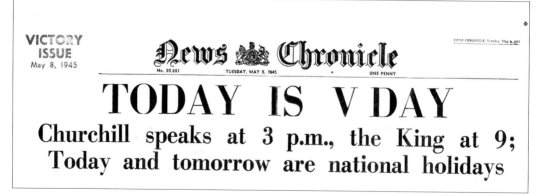

The Victory Issue of the News Chronicle *celebrating VE Day, 8 May 1945.*

A VE Day street party, Southall, May 1945.

A VE Day street procession, Southall, May 1945.

A mother and baby at a VE Day street party, Southall, May 1945.

A VE Day street party in Brentham, May 1945.

A children's VE Day street party in Glenfield Road, Ealing, May 1945.

There were similar gatherings in Acton and Southall. Bonfires blazed throughout Acton – the largest being on the allotments at Acton Vale – streets and houses were decorated, church bells rang and impromptu parties were the order of the day and, later in the week, hundreds of street parties were held. Acton, also, had its march past and service of thanksgiving in Acton Park on Sunday 13 May. Over 2,000 people assembled in the park and St Mary's church was crowded for a civic service of thanksgiving for victory.

In Southall, the newspaper reported fluttering flags, rosettes in coats, ribbons in hair, fancy hats on heads, cheerful crowds, dancing in the streets, roaring bonfires, burning effigies of Hitler and floodlit cinemas. The following days saw children's street parties, Victory dances and, more soberly, thanksgiving services in the churches. The main service of thanksgiving was also held on Sunday 13 May. The service was attended by representatives of all the Services and civil organisations who had paraded earlier through Southall and attracted a crowd of 4,000 people.

The diarist Erica Ford, on a late shift that day at her Fire Service canteen, saw the Ealing celebrations in the town centre. She wrote:

Tuesday May 8th, Victory Day: At last. Cycled to 'Z' via Broadway – houses and shops gay with bunting and flags & church bells ringing. Sunday routine – rather quiet at C1. Went to Hanger Lane for while.

Back for tea. Bacon roll for supper. We watched band go out and play outside Town Hall from 8.00 – 9.00. Bob Hallett was wanted as drum major at last minute. We all cheered it &

rushed to side entrance to watch & cheer it past. When band came marching back half of Ealing was marching behind & came right into the yard through the gates – wonderful sight. Band played some more, then dismissed.

Piano was brought down & chairs put in huge circle & dance band played & yard was floodlit. Very gay. Mrs Cook & her son came along. 'H' cycled up park & sat there for a while. Lovely warm night.

Houses floodlit & bonfires scenting the air. 'M' & 'D' got back from Jarvis's soon after me. We watched huge searchlight display weaving & remaining stationary.

'M' & I cycled round to have a look about 12.40. Couldn't get down Haven Lane because of crowd dancing outside pubs. Big crowd on The Green singing & dancing.

Had look at fire station, but they had finished. Cycled back via Hanger Lane. Bed 1.45.

John Cordon also captured the atmosphere of VE Day with the following description of his local Greenford celebration:

On the morning of VE Day the men strung up lots of union jacks and bunting and put up some trestle tables and benches for the party. Us lads built a massive bonfire outside no. 25. We got a bit carried away and by the time we finished it was about twelve foot high.

We all dressed up for the party. I was thirteen and had just got my first pair of long trousers – so I wore them. Somebody made up some paper hats with a 'V' on them – but I wouldn't wear one. After the party a photographer came and took a picture – the first photo of any of us for six years.

A children's VE Day street party in Chamberlain Road, May 1945.

A VE Day street party in Hessel Road, May 1945.

North Greenford Victory Queen,
sixteen-year-old Beryl Langford, in 1945.

When the tables were cleared away we had races and games for kids and grown-ups. One mum won a race but unfortunately the boys holding the finishing line didn't let go when she finished and she fell over.

It was a really hot day and they put some benches on the pavement under a big rowan tree, which was in this bloke's front garden, so that the old folks could sit in the shade. He came out and made them take the benches away. Nobody ever spoke to him again.

Of course we wanted to light the bonfire but they made us wait until it got a bit dark. When it was lit it really went up. At one point we thought we might have to call the fire brigade. It gave off a ferocious heat. Marvellous! A bit later on we put potatoes in the fire. They came out like charcoal but we still tried to eat them.

Then Mr Saville, the scrap merchant at no. 33, brought a piano out into the street. We didn't even know he had one, so you can imagine our surprise when he sat down and played anything we wanted by ear. We sang all the wartime songs – *Roll Out the Barrel, Run Rabbit, White Cliffs of Dover, We'll Meet Again* and so on – and people danced. Some of the young girls danced together. The boys were much too shy to dance with them so we poked fun at them by dancing with each other. We thought that was very funny. Then we did the Hokey Cokey several times and did the Conga up and down the road. It was a great atmosphere. Us lads kept putting more stuff on the fire to keep it going.

Victory tea party for St Peter's Road and Cornwall Avenue residents, Southall, August 1945.

I think it finished about midnight. I was still so excited I couldn't sleep. I kept getting up and looking out at the glowing embers of the fire, which was only a few yards from my window. The next morning it was just a pile of ashes. And so it was all over. Then we saw that it had burnt off all the tarmac on the road – a patch about twelve foot round. The council came and patched it up but you could still see the scar for years and years after.

A few days later the council came around and lit the gas street lamps. We just couldn't believe the amount of light they gave out. We rushed indoors to get comics and went into hysterics when we found that we could actually read them under the street light.

VJ Day

Japan surrendered on Wednesday 15 August 1945 – less than fourteen weeks after the defeat of Germany – and the world was at 'peace' again. The VJ Day celebrations were generally more muted than those of VE Day but were, nevertheless, heartfelt. Celebrations in the three boroughs did not really get under way until the evening and then very much followed the junketing in May.

Acton got off to a noisier start to the day. Sirens and hooters had sounded at midnight to announce the Japanese surrender but the pattern for the two-day holiday was then similar to that in Ealing.

VE Day street party held in Willow Road, South Ealing, August 1945.

A newspaper report on Southall was headed 'VJ Day in Southall Began with Queues and Ended with Bonfires'. There were queues for food, queues for cigarettes, queues for buses and a persistent drizzle. The rain cleared in the afternoon, the sun came out and so did the people, and by the evening the parties were in full swing.

VE Day and VJ Day in the three boroughs were days of public rejoicing and of private grief. It should also be noted that after happy celebrations and reunions the victory days and nights were, alas, to be followed by a lengthy period of austerity – with shortages of consumer goods and continued rationing of imported foodstuffs and petrol. The problems facing a tired people were enormous – massive reconstruction and repair, re-housing, attempts to restore traditional family life, reviving a battered economy and, at the same time, establishing the foundations of the promised welfare state. But at least the guns were silent.

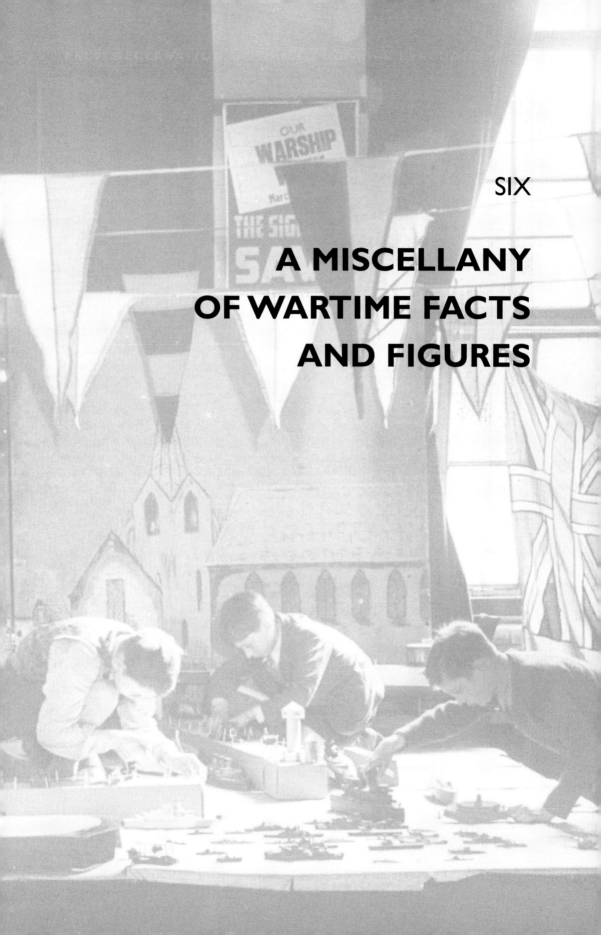

SIX

A MISCELLANY OF WARTIME FACTS AND FIGURES

Rationing

Wartime food rationing provided a nutritious, if monotonous diet, and, together with a big decrease in the consumption of sugar and fats, improved the health of the adult population. The green ration book which ensured a daily diet of milk and a double supply of eggs for pregnant women, nursing mothers and young children, plus day nurseries for the children of working mothers and school meals, similarly improved the health of the younger generation. The wartime story of improved health is a remarkable one.

Viewed from today, when obesity rather than malnutrition is of national concern, the basic food rations of the war years seem unbelievably meagre. Here are some facts and figures:

Food rationing began on 8 January 1940, with 4oz of ham, 4oz of bacon, 4oz of sugar and 4oz of butter per adult per week, and about half that for young children. In April 1940, Lord Woolton became Minister of Food; in July 1940, tea, margarine and cooking fats were rationed at 2oz per

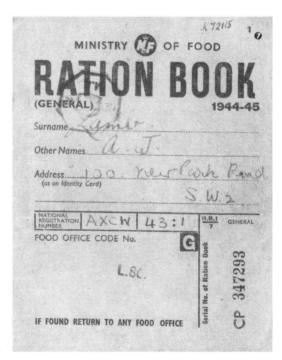

Ration book, issued in 1944.

week and cheese fluctuated between 2oz and 8oz per week; May 1941 saw cheese down to 1oz per week; July 1941 saw the introduction of clothes rationing and the controlled distribution of eggs; the controlled distribution of milk followed in November 1941 and, in December 1941, the points scheme was introduced to limit consumption of non-rationed goods.

1942 saw soap rationing (3oz per month); a reduced clothing ration; the end of white bread and the start of utility furniture. By the summer of 1943, petrol, fuel, blankets, beer and foodstuffs were very scarce. Coal rationing, at 4cwt per household per month, came in 1944 and whale meat and snoek (a kind of barracuda) appeared in the shops in 1945.

Victory in Europe saw the reduction of the bacon and lard rations and the clothing allowance was further reduced after the final victory over Japan. A final irony was that rationing in various forms continued in victorious Britain well into the years of peace.

Food rationing ensured the fairest possible distribution of the food supply across the whole population, but one group at least often felt hungry – the large numbers of boys and girls in the urban areas. Pauline Clift in her wartime recollections describes the situation most clearly:

> Getting some variety into our diets was an endless task for our mothers. We talked a lot about food, what we would eat 'after the war'; whether it was worth queuing up at Sainsbury's for two hours in case there was some offal, such as liver, kidneys, even tripe, which we tried once; whether we'd ever see bananas again.
>
> Sometimes a shipload of oranges got through the blockade at sea, but they were often reserved for children. I seem to remembering sharing mine. There was a wonderful shop which sold hand-made chocolate on one of the streets leading from the main road to Walpole Park (I forget the name: Bond Street? High Street? Main Street? It was the one where the Walpole cinema stood). We discussed whether to blow our sweets rations for a month, I believe it was, on four chocolates. The good part of all that was that many of us who were children then still have a full set of teeth.
>
> During the war, the school milk scheme was introduced. We had free milk every day. My working mother, like so many others, had to rush out each morning, leaving us to fend for ourselves. Without the free milk, and three Peak Frean's biscuits for 3d, we would have had no breakfast at all. As it was, I was always so hungry that I could barely think before 10.00 a.m., when the bell went for break.
>
> Families were bombarded with information on good nutrition: carrots for our eyes: well, there were few other veggies. Going into the greengrocer's was a depressing exercise. By the end of winter there was nothing to buy except potatoes, carrots and cooked beets.
>
> But we had rose-hip jelly for Vitamin C and a viscous and a gooey caramel-tasting concoction laced with Vitamin D. As George Orwell noted, average Britons had never been better nourished.

The black-out

All who experienced it will remember the black-out, which was rigorously enforced. It produced a feeling of safety from questing enemy bombers, but many people found it frightening and it led to a sharp increase in crime and road-accident fatalities. In the early weeks of the war, black-out paper was made available – reinforced black, brown or grey paper which could be tacked over windows until proper curtains were made. Two thicknesses of paper were placed over side and rear lights of motor vehicles. Headlight reflectors were removed or painted over and solid cardboard masks, with a one inch-diameter hole in the centre, were fitted.

Most interior light bulbs were removed from buses, trams, trolley buses and trains and the remaining bulbs, together with the top half of windows, were covered in a dark blue, transparent paint. Passengers were bathed in a ghastly glow. White paint appeared on kerbs and on other hazardous objects in an effort to give some guidance to pedestrians and drivers in the black-out.

Torches were in huge demand and there was a shortage of batteries. Eventually, only no. 8 and U2 batteries reached the shops – sometimes. Remedies to prolong the life of batteries including warming them in the oven!

Petrol

Petrol supply was an obvious problem and 'pool' petrol (low grade) and rationing were introduced. The basic allowance was based upon horse-power and some private motoring was possible but this was eventually done away with. The commercial allowance was based upon business requirements and individual requirements were determined by users' associations e.g. the National Farmers Union.

Other measures

The carrying of gas masks and identity cards was compulsory in 1939, but the carrying of gas masks was abandoned later.

Glass protection also assumed great importance in 1939. Panes of glass were protected by crisscrossing them with gummed paper (to prevent splintering) – a practice which ended in private houses in 1940 but which continued in public buildings.

The threat of invasion was very real in 1940. Signposts and railway station name boards were removed and road blocks and pill-boxes were erected at strategic points throughout the country during the summer months.

Anti-aircraft defences

The value of the anti-aircraft defences lay not so much in shooting down enemy aircraft as in the prevention of accurate bombing. Anti-aircraft gunfire compelled the German planes to fly at a higher altitude and effectively interfered with their ability to keep a straight and even course, and in this the guns were reinforced by the barrage balloons. Bursting shells and searchlights also indicated the positions of enemy aircraft to British fighters.

Two main types of gun were employed – the 4.5in, which could hurl a high explosive shell to a height of eight miles, and the much more numerous 3.7in gun, which had a faster rate of fire and used a smaller shell. Locating aircraft and charting their intended courses were assisted by the Vickers Predictor (a calculating machine) and the height finder.

Later in the war, the advent of the radar-controlled gun and the proximity-fused shell made the AA defences more lethal and the guns began to take a heavy toll on the enemy and airborne radar similarly increased the effectiveness of the night fighter.

There were three static gun site locations in or near the three boroughs and these formed a segment of the Inner Artillery Zone (IAZ) of the gun defences of the London Region. The sites were at Wormwood Scrubs, Gunnersbury Park and Brentham Meadows and their impact on the district was often referred to by local diarists. The sites were not always occupied and apart from playing their full part in the general AA barrage in the autumn of 1940, were at their most effective during the 'baby blitz' of 1944 when the enemy raiders approached central London from the west and north-west. The noisiest and most alarming weapon would seem to have been the 5.5in gun sited at Wormwood Scrubs in 1943. This gun hurled an 80lb shell up to a height of 43,000ft and made a fearsome noise in the process. Twin-barrelled rocket guns added to the cacophony, often to the great alarm of friend and foe alike.

The development of airborne radar (AI) has a direct local connection. The only English Heritage blue plaque to be seen in Ealing (on a house in The Ridings) honours the work of Alan Dower Blumlein, a noted electronics engineer and inventor, who was responsible for many major developments in telecommunications, television and radar. His work in the development of airborne radar was crucial and his contribution to the defence of this country vital. Sadly, Mr Blumlein died in an air crash in 1942 whilst engaged in testing another device, the H2S system, for RAF Bomber Command.

The Home Guard

On 10 May 1940 the Germans invaded France and the Low Countries and advanced rapidly with their armoured divisions and paratroops. Four days later, alarmed by the spectre of a German airborne invasion of Britain, the War Minister, Anthony Eden, asked for volunteers for a force to be called the Local Defence Volunteers (LDV). The first recruit turned up within four minutes of the broadcast and a great civilian army, unarmed and without uniforms and organisation at first, evolved into the Home Guard. By 1943 it was nearly two million strong, had cadres of regular serving members, had taken over many duties from the army – including manning anti-aircraft rocket batteries – and was increasingly professional. It was disbanded on 2 December 1944.

In our district, a Home Guard guerilla training school was established in Osterley Park and all the local units engaged in exercises ranging from full-scale battle exercises to anti-gas training. A number of local factories had their own Home Guard units.

Middlesex Home Guard: 3 Platoon, 'D' Company, 16th Battalion.

Home Guard on defensive exercise at Rockware Glass factory.

Maj. Bisgood and Col. E.J. King inspecting Home Guard on Ealing Common, August 1940.

The invasion of Britain, of course, never came, but had it done so the western part of the London inner defence line which ran along the river Brent, was to be manned by units of the regular army. Our local Home Guard units would then have had a vital role to play in the defence of the country.

The civilian defenders

The defenders – civil and military – loom large in memories of the war years. Civil defence was not restricted to the Air Raid Wardens. Also under the banner of 'civil defence' were control and communications personnel; ambulance, First Aid Post and stretcher party personnel; rescue party, gas decontamination, demolition, shelter warden and road and sewer repair personnel. Civil defence activities were numerous and encompassed test centres, evacuation, re-housing, house requisitioning and casualty enquiries. One must also remember the police and their auxiliaries who in many areas were the lynch-pin of civil defence; the boy and girl messengers; the vital hospital and emergency services, Red Cross and St John Ambulance members and, of course, the National Fire Service, created in August 1941. This great civilian army did not fail us when the test came.

Of the military defenders, one thinks immediately of the brave members of the bomb disposal units of the Royal Engineers and of the Royal Navy.

Firefighters in Hessel Road, carrying out community defence.

Mobilisation and demobilisation

One cannot think of the impact of war on the civilian population without referring to the mobilisation (call-up), and subsequent demobilisation (demob), of several million British men and women during the war years.

The first measure in the mobilisation of men during the Second World War was the Military Training Act of March 1939. Conscription of men aged twenty and twenty-one for six months' military training with the armed services was introduced. Reservists were called up on 24 August, and on 3 September 1939 men aged between eighteen and forty-one years were made liable for call-up under the National Service Act of that date. Men aged forty years did not register until June 1941.

In March 1941, women were asked to volunteer for war work – particularly in industry – and from December 1941, unmarried women and childless widows, aged from nineteen to thirty years, were liable for call-up for the forces. By October 1942, all women up to forty-five years had been called for interview regarding war work and this process was extended to women in the forty-six to fifty years age bracket in 1943. By the end of 1943, over 400,000 women were in the women's services, in the ATS, WAAF or WRNS, and several millions more were in war work.

Details of the plans for demobilisation were released by the government in September 1944. There were two classes. Class 'B' covered builders and others required for post-war reconstruction. They would have priority of release, but would be recalled if they left the work to which they had been directed. Class 'A' covered the remainder of the conscripted servicemen and for them the release date would be determined by age and by length of service.

There was much personal rejoicing at the prospect of the demobilisation of several million servicemen and women, and the first 200,000 were released in June 1945, before the Japanese surrendered in August.

In Sue McAlpine's *Voices of Ealing and Hounslow*, John Hearn gives a moving account of his long demob journey from the Far East to his home in Chiswick. Mr Hearn embarked in Singapore in November 1946, landed at Liverpool and finally reached his demob centre at Woking. He writes:

We were given our demob clothes, a suit, hat, shoes, tie and underclothes and the first good meal we'd had in a long time of bacon, sausages, eggs and fresh bread, a smashing breakfast! My mates and I said our farewells, not knowing if we would ever meet again... With all our gear issued we were taken by lorry to Woking Station to catch a train to Waterloo and from there told to make our own way home. By this time I was well and truly loaded up with baggage! I had all my army gear in a big solid demob box, a kit bag that was packed tight with tinned fruit, a big heavy tin box with presents for all the family, with cigarettes, clothes, (which included the beautiful Chinese-style silk pyjama suit for Mary); all gifts which I had bought in Singapore, and they weighed a ton!

When we reached Waterloo, with another chap who lived in Heathfield Terrace, I struggled in quite heavy rain onto a local train that took us to Grove Park Station in Chiswick. I unloaded all my bags and boxes and then carried them in stages to the bus stop outside, from where we caught a no. 55 bus. We had a job to fit everything onto the bus but the conductor was very good, letting us pack it underneath the stairs and wait there with it, saying nothing was too much trouble for soldiers returning from the war. He stopped along Heathfield Terrace for the other chap to get off, then took the bus right to the top of Holly Road and helped me unload all my gear. I shall never forget that day, the rain by then was pouring down so hard is seemed as if the heavens had opened up, everywhere looked drab and grey but to me it looked the most wonderful sight in the world. I was lumbered up with all that luggage and so short of breath that when I got halfway down Holly Road, I left the big tin box and the valise in the middle of the pavement and ran down with the rest to knock on the door of no. 19. I threw the things down on the doorstep, ran back and picked up the box and valise and as I ran back to the house, there was Joyce ... every bit as beautiful as I remembered.

A quiet day in Northolt

There is a tendency to think that the daytime battle with the Luftwaffe in the summer of 1940 had been won by the RAF by early September, and that when the night blitz began on 7 September there was little enemy activity during the day. This was not the case, as the following culled from the log of the J4 Wardens' Post, Northolt, for Sunday 27 October 1940, shows:

Sunday 27 October came and went in the middle of an air raid. The sirens which had sounded on the Saturday evening had heralded the fiftieth consecutive heavy night raid on London. The night was noisy with gunfire but there were no incidents in J4's district and the relief when the 'All Clear' sounded at 07.00 hours on that Sunday morning was genuine enough.

By now, the most widespread feeling was not one of anxiety but one of infinite weariness, coupled with the hope of a restful Sunday ahead. But it was not to be. At 07.50 hours the sirens wailed again and the red alert lasted for two hours. No bombs fell. At 10.55 an unexploded anti-aircraft shell was reported at the rear of no. 294 Church Road, and the police and central control were informed. Mid-morning and the church services began – prayers seemed more heartfelt in those days – but were interrupted at 11.30 by the second alert of the day. All quiet; all clear again at 12.10; a sense of relief and signs of normal life being resumed. Then, within eight minutes, another red alert at 12.18 for forty minutes or so but again, no bombs, no incidents. Then more alerts from 13.37 to 14.18 and from 16.42 to 17.35, followed by thoughts of the coming night. Would they come again – for the fifty-first night running? They did. The sirens moaned again at 18.50 for another heavy raid on London and this alert lasted for eleven hours forty minutes – until 06.20 on Monday 28 October.

Sunday 27 October 1940, a 'quiet' day in Northolt.

Some common memories of the Blitz, 1940/41

Individual reactions to the bombing differ widely but some memories are shared; of vapour trails in the sky, of distant gunfire and of sirens. Nights when the searchlights coned overhead and the bombing moved westwards over the three boroughs. Heart-stopping moments when the bombs hurtled down, rending the air; when the earth trembled and when the glare of incendiary bombs penetrated blacked-out homes and shelters and, in the wake of the bombing, the distinctive smells of bombed buildings – of leaking gas and of damp plaster. But, above all, in that grim autumn and winter, the growing sense of exhaustion. But there were no thoughts of giving in; there was no talk of surrender.

Some unexpected features of the air raids

The fact that there were far fewer casualties than expected in relation to the physical damage.
The large amount of rescue, repair and clearance work needed.
The large number of unexploded bombs (and shells) which required temporary evacuation.
The need for reinforcement – in hard-hit districts or towns.
The sheer number of incidents in heavy raids which caused problems in reporting and in directing the rescue services, and so on.
The problems of locating casualties in intense darkness.
The extensive welfare services needed after the raids.
The use of V1 flying bombs and V2 rockets.
The widespread bombing of rural areas and coastal villages thought to be safe.
The use of the parachute mine.
Fires were more damaging than explosions.
The number of casualties in the ranks of the Fire Services, Police and Civil Defence services; 793 firemen and twenty-five firewomen were killed, and over 7,000 were injured in the UK raids.
The widespread damage to hospitals – hundreds were damaged throughout the UK.

Luftwaffe target, AEC Southall, September 1940.

Local industries at war

The greatest expansion of wartime industry in London came in west and north-west London where the industrial boom of the inter-war years had produced large, modern, well-equipped factories. Typical local examples were Hoover, A.E.C. and C.A.V. The demand for labour was met in various ways. Many unmarried women were directed into war work and moved to areas like Acton, and many men in essential war occupations moved from the heavily-bombed areas of east and south east London to west and north-west London generally. The contribution to the war effort of factories of all sizes in Ealing, Acton and Southall cannot be overestimated. A few examples must suffice.

A.E.C., in Southall, switched from making buses to producing armoured cars with six-pounder guns. A total of about 5,000 new employees were recruited and the range of wartime products was extended. In all the company produced 8,600 Matador trucks; 3,250 diesel engines for Valentine tanks and nearly 400 for Matilda tanks; 150 fully-armoured vehicles which served as battle headquarters for military commanders in the front line and large numbers of power units for generators and dockside cranes, and the list of wartime artefacts does not end there.

The history of the A.E.C. factory relates, for example, how its servicing department dealt with an unprecedented volume of work during the five-and-a-half years of war. Luftwaffe maps showing the factory clearly delineated attested to its importance as a target and the factory was duly hit:

On the night of September 24 1940, the Southall Service Department was struck by a bomb which put a large part of the building out of action for six months. Happily, workers on the nightshift had taken cover in nearby shelters and not a single man was injured. Damage to the building, however, was extensive, the explosion having wrecked the roof, blown out windows and doors, uprooted machine tools and rendered many vehicles un-repairable.

At the time over 700 separate jobs were in hand, but luckily all correspondence and documents relating thereto escaped destruction so that every order could be completed, apart from the vehicles that had to be written off as having disappeared 'without trace'.

A great amount of additional work was caused by some of the curious effects of the blast. For example, examination of several gear boxes, undamaged externally, revealed that many of the gear teeth had disappeared. In another instance, a rear axle was opened up in search of glass when it was found that four of the bevel pinions were split in half. As the result of these and similar strange happenings, every unit and sub-unit became suspect and had to be examined or stripped before it could be released for service.

In addition to dealing with unpredictable defects, the service work went on under supremely difficult conditions; vehicles were overhauled in odd corners of the main factory while units were dismantled and reconditioned wherever cover could be found.

For many weeks the service mechanics worked at their machines and benches, exposed to every wind that blew, and with only a tarpaulin overhead to protect them from the rain. During the severe winter of 1940, nothing better than temporarily installed braziers could be used for internal heating, and all work had to finish immediately at the hour of blackout.

Added to this were repeated air-raid warnings, sometimes as many as eight in twenty-four hours, yet notwithstanding all these hard conditions, the service went on and as a result of steadfast efforts, willingness and co-operation of the depot personnel – men and women alike – A.E.C. traditions of service were maintained at the highest possible level.

The story of the Hoover factory at war is even more remarkable. The scale of Hoover war production was such that it could be claimed that scarcely a British aircraft or tank went into action without equipment of Hoover manufacture. A company diagram of a Halifax Bomber,

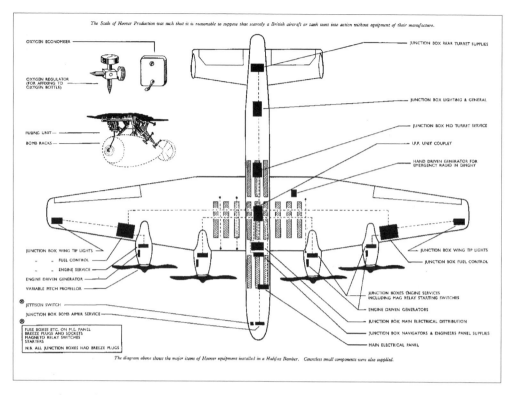

Diagram showing the major items of Hoover equipment installed in a Halifax Bomber.

showing the major items of Hoover equipment installed in the aircraft, proves how vital the components were. The plane would be grounded without them.

Napier, in Acton, produced aero-engines, including those for two very successful aircraft of the later war years – the Tempest and Typhoon. C.A.V. also switched to munitions production and Waring and Gillow, on the old Acton aerodrome site, were taken over by the Ministry of Aircraft Production and produced parts for the revolutionary aircraft – the Mosquito.

The output from the factories and workshops of the three boroughs was immense and so was the effort of the people involved, as the following example will show. In those desperate weeks in early summer 1940, when Britain stood alone, an appeal was made to people in the aircraft factories to work round the clock. Many did so but their extra efforts proved to be counter-productive for, after a few weeks total effort, reports from the aircraft factories, including Napier, showed that by the end of July 1940 many workers were exhausted and production was falling. A sixty hour week was then introduced throughout British industry.

London Transport at war

The record of London Transport during the war both in its primary role of transporting Londoners and as a major producer of munitions is a remarkable one. There were dozens of incidents involving damage to roads, rails, overhead wiring, tunnels and garages but LT, or rather the men and women of London Transport, carried on. A few of the major incidents will remind us of their problems. The Blitz months, beginning in September 1940, caused much dislocation in central and East London and there were constant diversions to bus, tram and trolley bus services due to craters, unexploded bombs or damage to overhead wiring and track. But the worst incidents were experienced on the underground where a number of stations were hit with loss of life. Seven people were killed at Trafalgar Square Station, nineteen at Bounds Green, sixty-four at Balham and 111 at Bank Station (on 11 January 1941). Other incidents were reported from Sloane Square and Moorgate stations. On 17 October 1940, an appeal was made for provincial buses and the regions responded immediately. Travel into central London from Ealing and Acton was dislocated on several occasions, for example, on the night of 19 April 1941 when the Central Line was closed between Wood Lane and Ealing Broadway and on 19 February 1944 when damaged bridges again caused closure between the same points. The District and Piccadilly line services were also interrupted on other occasions, including V1 damage at Ravenscourt Park and South Kensington.

Comment from London Transport staff illustrate the feelings of the time. One bus driver recalls that: 'Strangely enough, it seemed that people felt safer when travelling on a bus and they had every confidence in the driver. It helped us considerably to keep going when we continually got a "Goodnight, driver, and thank you".'
A 'clippie' (one of the hundreds of women conductors during the war years) remembers:

> One night we were on late turn and the sirens went. I lost my nerve and said to my driver, 'I'm not going'. There was a crowd of women and children on the bus and one woman said 'Ain't you going? What about us?' So we went and the moment we started my fear left me.

Equally heartwarming is the story of London Transport wartime production of aircraft, tanks and munitions. The Acton works made armoured vehicles and repaired damaged ones; overhauled, tested and repaired landing-craft motors and generators for the Admiralty and rebuilt railway wagons for the Southern Railway. They also made torpedo boat engine bases and canopies; noses for naval shells; caterpillar frames for excavating machines; equipped bridge-laying tanks and then converted tanks to operate in water up to 10ft deep, and all this was only a part of their war work.

Savings, salvage and slogans

The pattern of life in Britain changed very little during the second half of the war. Austerity prevailed with restrictions, and shortages were a constant feature. Rationing, however, although occasionally adjusted to meet contingencies, was not extended.

Slogans reinforcing government strictures monopolised most urban advertising hoardings and, of these, the most numerous were those exhorting the people to save. Their savings, it was claimed, helped to finance the war effort although the main purpose of the savings campaign was, in fact, to dampen inflation. Nevertheless, the National Savings movement was vigorously supported throughout the community. Savings drives were staged throughout the country, often with a special theme – 'Wings for Victory', 'Salute the Soldier', 'War Weapons Week', 'Warships Week' and so on (a Spitfire was said to cost £5,000 and communities and companies hastened to have their own named aircraft). Savings certificates – 15s – or stamps were often the prizes in social and competitive events. Everybody, it was said, from the very young to the very old, could do their bit to help the war effort by saving. The shortage of consumer goods also boosted the campaign and most households held some savings certificates. Workers in many industries connected with war production were earning good wages but found little of value to buy. The increase in incomes and income tax also greatly increased the flow of cash into the national coffers. Purchase Tax, introduced in 1941, was not levied on food and other essentials and with a top rate of 33% increased that flow further.

The war years also saw an early version of today's accent on recycling – although not for today's 'green' reasons. The wartime campaign of salvage was, in fact, another kind of saving but in this case of material things. Jam jars, bottles, envelopes, wrapping paper and string were among the articles to be saved for re-use. If a use could not be found in your own home, the waste went for salvage. Paper was collected for re-pulping, leather for fertilizer, bones made bone meal, glue or explosives, and rags could be reclaimed for yarn. Kitchen waste was also collected and processed into what Londoners called 'Tottenham Pudding,' for pig feed.

The collection of salvage was mostly done on a voluntary basis by organisations like the Women's Voluntary Service or the Boy Scouts. Further, people were asked to part with household articles which were made of scarce and valuable metals, notably aluminium. The patriotic cast out teapots and saucepans, ostensibly to help build aircraft, but disillusion grew with reports that the heaps of discarded pots and pans remained untouched. There was similar displeasure at the loss of cast-iron railings from public and private buildings and parks, which had been compulsorily removed. One Ealing man who had sacrificed his ornamental front gate was incensed on seeing it still in a builder's yard eighteen months later. If enthusiasm for salvage waned, there is evidence that the collections did prove to be an important reserve and were resorted to periodically.

In addition to savings and salvage, frugality was the keynote elsewhere in the wartime household. No hand washing under running taps, no more than five inches of water in the bath, no more leaving an electric light bulb switched on in an empty room, and so on. And, finally, if venturing from hearth and home, the citizen was likely to be confronted with the slogan, 'Is Your Journey Really Necessary?'

A sale held at Costons School during Warships Week, March 1942.

Opposite: *Southall division of the British Red Cross process to the Town Hall during War Weapons Week, May 1941.*

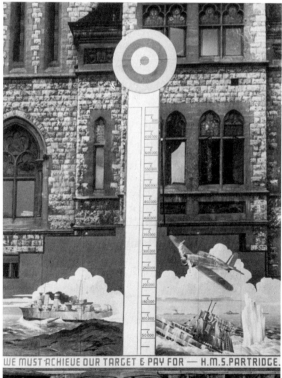

Above: *A Naval balloon promoting Warships Week, in Ealing, March 1942.*

Left: *Target for Ealing's Warships Week, March 1942.* HMS Partridge *was destroyed by enemy action in 1943.*

Air Marshal Maynard makes a speech during Wings for Victory Week, West Ealing, March 1943.

Stamped bomb in Dean Gardens, Wings for Victory Week, March 1943.

Overleaf: *Wings for Victory parade, Walpole Park, Ealing, March 1943.*

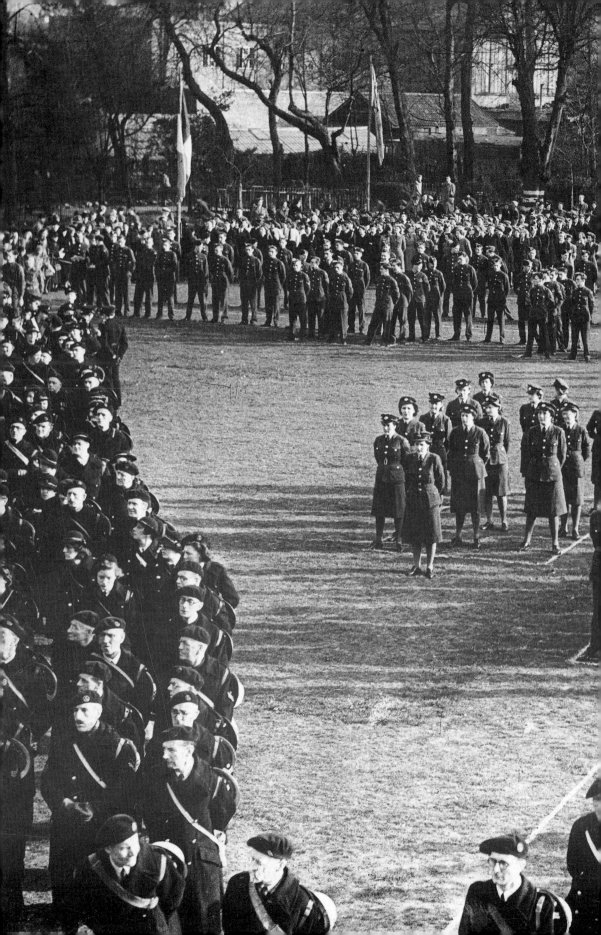

Official opening of Salute the Soldier week in Walpole Park by Lt-Gen. Sir Douglas Brownrigg, Ealing, March 1944.

German First World War gun to be melted down for salvage.

Southall held a 'salvage fortnight' in September 1941. This float was part of the inaugural procession which was a mile-and-a-half in length and followed a route from Adelaide Road to Southall Park.

A 'salvage fortnight' float, Southall, September 1941.

Pigswill promotion float in the 'salvage fortnight' procession, September 1941.

Salvage collection, Ealing, 1940.

Opposite: *Greenford, allotments drive, 1940.*

Entertainment in wartime: The wireless, the pictures and Ealing studios

The role of the radio and the cinema – the wireless and the pictures – to inform and entertain was crucial during the war years. Newspapers, although vital, were very restricted in scope and in content – shortage of newsprint and rigid censorship saw to that.

The BBC achieved its great national and international reputation then. Speech and music reigned supreme and, for the first time in history, correspondents could bring the sounds of war direct from the battle fronts. They were the years of the great Churchill broadcasts and of broadcasters like J.B. Priestley and the gifted American, Quentin Reynolds. They were the years of the Forces Programme and the Home Service and, if they gave us ITMA and Workers' Playtime, they also gave us the Brains Trust and splendid music.

As for the cinema, going to the pictures in those pre-television years (the limited television service closed down in 1939) was almost a national pastime with the exception of the very young and the very old. They were the golden years of cinema attendance and Hollywood escapism was a godsend. They were also good years for the British film industry, in spite of wartime difficulties, and Ealing Studios played a major part in the increased prestige which resulted from the many, good wartime British films. Cinemas, like theatres, were closed for a few days on the outbreak of war and then suffered severely from bombing. Sixty cinemas were destroyed in the London area and many more were damaged.

Ealing Studios was also damaged by bombing. A direct hit destroyed stage number two and some work was transferred to Wembley as a result, but the output never wavered. It could in fact be argued that of all the vital articles of war which flowed from the factories and workshops of Ealing, Acton and Southall, none was more vital to the well-being of the British people than the films produced by Ealing Studios.

The women of London, 1939-45

Many tributes have been paid to the women of Britain but none better than that delivered by J.B. Priestley in his radio broadcast on the evening of 22 September 1940. Mr Priestley was speaking at the height of the Blitz and said, amongst other things:

> It is ten times harder being a decent wife and mother during such a war than it is being a soldier. You have to make a far greater effort to keep going, for you've no training and discipline to armour you. The soldier has his own responsibilities, but when he assumed them he was released from a great many others, whereas his womenfolk know no such release, but have more and more responsibility heaped upon them.
>
> And they needn't even be wives and mothers. Nothing has impressed me more in this battle of London than the continued high courage and resolution, not only of the wives and mothers but also of the crowds of nurses, secretaries, clerks, telephone girls, shop assistants and waitresses who, morning after morning, have turned up for duty neat as ever – rather pink about the eyes, perhaps, and smiling rather tremulously, but still smiling ... a lot of London girls – pale-faced little creatures living on cups of tea and buns – defy this Goering and all his Luftwaffe and all their high explosives and incendiaries and machine guns, and carry on, still trim and smiling. Isn't that a triumph?

And, as we know, amongst those much-admired ranks were women and girls from Ealing, Acton and Southall.

Greenford ladies mending clothes for the children of women war workers.

Women's War Work Bureau at Eastern's, West Ealing, November 1941.

Mayoress Mrs Ada Garner (left), with Mrs Catu and Mrs Watts at Ealing garments collection.

*Land Army girls
gathering potatoes
at Greenford.*

*Mayor Willoughby
Garner 'lends a
hand on the land'.*

The children of Britain

Early in 1941, a special religious service was broadcast for the 'children of Britain' and the
following quotation from the Book of Revelations was made in respect of the many children
who had been killed in the air attacks: 'And God shall wipe away all tears from their eyes; and
there shall be no more death, neither sorrow, nor crying, neither shall there by any more pain;
for the former things are passed away.' (Rev 21:3, 4).

A *Marie Celeste* of the skies?

The first four months of 1944 saw a resumption of heavy air raids on London, and the Germans, now confronted by the strongest defence in the world, tried to approach the capital from the north west. By doing this, they subjected the people of the three boroughs to some of the loudest and most alarming raids of the war.

A night raid on 23 February 1944 produced a very remarkable incident. A Dornier 217 bomber, carrying one 1,000kg and two 500kg high explosive bombs, found itself coned by searchlights over Ealing and was immediately fired on by an anti-aircraft rocket battery. The crew, temporarily blinded and deafened by the exploding rockets, were convinced that their aircraft had been seriously damaged and baled out over Acton. Their aircraft, however, was largely undamaged and headed north eastwards, slowly descending. The plane eventually made a smooth belly-landing sixty miles or so from Acton in some allotments on the outskirts of the city of Cambridge. The Cambridge police and Home Guard were quickly on the scene and, understandably, were baffled by the arrival of an undamaged enemy bomber with no crew but plenty of fuel and a full bomb-load.

Fortune smiled on many people that night – firstly on the German crew and then on the thousands of people under the plane's flight path from Ealing to Cambridge.

Parcels for prisoners

The *Middlesex County Times* and *West Middlesex Gazette* reported on 26 May 1945 that the Prisoner of War Packing Centre at the Drill Hall in Featherstone Road, Southall, had finished its work. In five years, the packers had dispatched, via the Red Cross and St John, no fewer than 924,878 parcels, containing 15,722,926 commodities and had used 1,470 miles of string in the process. The standard parcel included butter, chocolate, a tin of Nestles [*sic*] full cream and a steak and kidney pudding. The effect on the health and morale of the prisoners who received them was incalculable.

Interestingly, the centre helped India House for a time to pack parcels for Indian prisoners of war and these parcels contained Atta (a form of flour), curry, biscuits and dhal. 510,699 of these parcels were dispatched from Southall and six repatriated Indian servicemen, passing through London on their way home, called at the centre to thank the helpers personally for the 'life-parcels', as they called them.

On reflection, no wartime products of industrious Southall were as vital or as welcome as these parcels.

The secret prisoner of Southall

In May 1941, Rudolf Hess, deputy leader of the Nazi party, astonished the world when he flew to Scotland. On his removal to London, he was secretly held for questioning in a house near Southall Park.

When Acton jumped the gun

'The Germans have surrendered'. This announcement flashed on the screen at the Savoy Cinema, East Acton, on Wednesday 2 May 1945, and set the organist playing *God Save the King* and *Land of Hope and Glory* and the audience dancing in the aisles.

The deputy manager then walked on to the stage and having – with difficulty – stopped the organist and quieted the general rejoicing, explained that the announcement written on the slide was 'The Germans have surrendered in Italy' but the slide, unfortunately, had slipped.

The return of the evacuees to Ealing

With the end of the war in Europe, the chairman of the Ealing Education Committee reported that the remaining 708 evacuees would be returning to Ealing. These evacuees would be returning from twenty-four counties, from Northumberland to Cornwall and Wales, and from over sixty places ranging in size from the city of Birmingham to remote Lake District villages, and from places as socially varied as the Rhondda Valley and Henley-on-Thames.

Never in the history of Ealing can its citizens have been so widely dispersed and been so thankful for it.

The ordeal on the Home Front

By May 1945 central London had experienced 1,224 air-raid warnings; suffered 352 air raids by night and by day and endured months of attack by flying bombs and rockets.

The material damage inflicted on the British people was enormous and to that should be added the physical effects – lack of sleep; hurried or interrupted meals; noise, dirt and bad ventilation; fear; greater risk of infection and of communicable disease; more deaths through accidents in the black-out, factory and home; more accidents to the young and to the elderly; and the social problems caused by separation – husbands from wives and children from parents.

Some recent reminders of war

Unexploded missiles still turn up occasionally to remind us of the Second World War. The latest one, locally, was reported in *The Gazette* of 13 May 1988 and led to the evacuation of 100 people from Keats Way, Greenford. The shell was safely detonated under a pile of sandbags by bomb disposal experts and the evacuees then returned to their homes. One wonders how many more bombs and shells are waiting to be exposed.

Another fairly recent reminder of war came in the wake of the Great Gale of October 1987. It was not just the howling wind, the crashing trees and the sound of breaking glass that stirred some memories but the fact that in some areas in our borough, fallen trees were found to contain bomb shrapnel and so could not be sawn up for commercial purposes.

GLOSSARY

A WARTIME ALPHABET

W hilst no record of wartime life can be really comprehensive, the following alphabetical list of wartime events, experiences, facts and figures should help create a picture of life on the Home Front in those dangerous years.

A is for Air Raid Precautions (ARP), air-raid warnings, air raids and air-raid casualties. Fear of air attacks had grown with the re-militarisation of Germany, under Hitler, in the thirties. Accordingly, in November 1938, Sir John Anderson was put in charge of ARP and evacuation plans. By early 1939, over one and a half million men and women had volunteered for civil defence duties – over one million of whom were unpaid.

The model citizen, we were told, would have completed the following by the outbreak of war: he would have turned one room into a gas-proof chamber; his windows and doors would emit no speck of light when night fell and glass panes would have been taped to lessen the effects of bomb blast; a spade, a bucket of sand and a bath full of water would stand ready to deal with fire-bombs and fires, and the family gas masks would be positioned ready for instant use. As an additional precaution – and before shelters became available in urban areas – he would have excavated an 11ft deep dug-out in his garden, complete with dimmed electric light. He would, in fact, be ready for any emergency. Needless to say, such paragons were few!

The air-raid warnings were usually sounded by sirens and by factory and colliery hooters in the urban and industrial areas – sounds can still awaken old fears. In addition, there were many more preliminary warnings (for example 'yellow' and 'purple' ones) which forewarned the civil defenders but which did not develop into public ('red') warnings. The air-raid warnings were not always followed by bombs and, sadly, bombs were not always preceded by sirens.

The total number of civilian air-raid casualties in the United Kingdom, including the lightly injured, was in excess of 300,000 – of which some 60,500 were killed.

'A' is also for animals. Many animals had to be put down in the aftermath of the raids. For example, in Hull, after the heavy raids in May 1941, the manager of the Dogs' Home dealt with some 600 animals in or near bombed premises – including dozens of dogs and cats, sixty-two birds, fifty-five pigs, forty-seven rabbits, ten chickens, two fish, two parrots and one monkey. One of the parrots – clearly a patriotic bird – thanked him by singing *Rule Britannia*.

B is for Bundles for Britain, British Restaurants, British Summer Time – and then Double British Summer Time – and, of course, the BBC. They were the years of the wireless; of the Home Service and the Forces' Programme, of ITMA, Music While You Work, The Radio Doctor, The Brains Trust and Sandy's Half Hour. They were also the days of the Kitchen Front with ingenious wartime recipes; carrot jam, cheese and potato custard, crow, mock fish, mock haggis, marrow surprise, oatmeal and herb sausages, sardine pancake, mock plum pudding, hard roe butter, rook pie with figgy paste, sparrow pie, and so on.

They were also the times when J.B. Priestley gave his 'Postscripts' after the nine o'clock news on Sunday evenings. His first postscript was on 5 June 1940, and then continued throughout that grim autumn and winter. They were broadcast at peak listening time, attracted a vast audience in Britain and overseas, and the calm, warm voice was well received wherever it was heard. The popularity of the broadcasts was largely due to the fact that in J.B. Priestley was a rare and happy fusion of writer, humanitarian and natural broadcaster.

C is for children, church bells, Churchill, cinemas and community spirit.

For too many children the war was a calamity but for many others (including the author), the war was not a bad time in which to grow up. True, sweets were rationed and school meals were pretty grim but there was excitement, occasional fear and less discipline with fathers in the Forces and mothers in essential war work. There were aircraft spotting sessions and collecting shrapnel and incendiary bomb fins for the boys, whilst the girls often became 'little women' with increased responsibilities in the home, with knitting 'comforts', with collecting salvage, and so on. But there was a darker side to this picture – many believe that the seeds of the burgeoning, post-war juvenile delinquency were sown in the war years.

Church bells were silenced except for invasion or, later, for victories.

Winston Churchill made many inspiring speeches and broadcasts, particularly his first broadcast as Prime Minister on 24 May 1940, which drew the following comment from a civil servant: 'The effect of that broadcast was magical. A confused and frightened people became courageous, hopeful and determined to see it through and no-one slipped back to the defeatism that disgraced the country from Munich to May'. A view shared by most Britons. In Winston Churchill, the hour had produced the man.

Cinemas, like theatres, closed for a short period, but had a massive business entertaining, informing and exhorting the British people.

On to community spirit. The pursuit of war brings grief and suffering to millions and shames mankind. Yet, ironically, war also produces widespread feelings of common purpose and comradeship – qualities which seem to elude us in the years of peace. Nor, in modern war, are these feelings restricted to the men and women of the armed services; during the Second World War, they were fully shared by the people on the Home Front. Perhaps this explains why the years between 1939 and 1945 are vividly recalled by so many of the people who lived through them.

D is for defenders. The following two stories come from two local defenders – one civil, one military. The first comes from a warden who, weary after a week of warnings (or alerts as they came to be called) and of bombs, was dozing on his feet. He was startled on hearing a voice calling urgently, 'Is there a warden anywhere?' The warden, now fully awake, located the person behind the voice only to be asked the immortal question: 'Any fish and chip shops open tonight, lad?' The warden's reply went unrecorded.

The second story comes from a gunner from Acton, who, as part of a searchlight unit, had just been moved to the middle of a moor:

At last my longed-for night off arrived. I shaved for the second time … put on my best battle dress, the trousers of which had been under my palliasse for days, and set off to sample a little night life once more. We had seen no-one during the three or four days we had been there and so our knowledge of local geography, with special reference to local hostelries, was vague. Knowing that we had come in a northerly direction on deployment from civilisation, I reasoned that if I walked south I should find civilisation again and catch a bus. After forty-five minutes' brisk walking without a sign of life, I came across a man trimming a hedge. I enquired of him: (a) the whereabouts of the nearest town; (b) of the nearest pub, and (c) what time the last bus went? I received the following astounding replies: (a) twelve miles, (b) six miles, and (c) Wednesday.

E is for evacuation, emergency water tanks in city streets, and for exhortations. Do you remember the exhortations? 'Dig for Victory', 'Careless Talk Costs Lives', 'Is Your Journey Really Necessary?' and a hundred others.

F is for friendliness, furniture (utility), fire-watching, fatigue and fear.

G is for gas masks (issued in 1938), and gas attacks.

H is for holidays-at-home, farm-working holidays, humour (never far below the surface), the Home Guard, the health of the nation, and housing. The loss of housing, temporarily or permanently, by enemy action, was a severe blow. By 1945, several million homes had been destroyed or damaged in varying degree by bombs, flying bombs and rockets.

I is for identity cards and invasion preparations.

J is for William Joyce (Lord Haw Haw); the German propagandist widely listened to despite appeals to the British people not to do so. Joint production committees in factories were a major step towards postwar joint consultation in industry.

K is for knitting (how many acres were produced by the women and girls of Britain for the forces, the bombed-out, the refugees etc?)

L is for literature. It has been said that, unlike the First World War, the Second World War did not produce any great war poets. Perhaps not, but some good poetry was written, and none was more popular than Squadron Leader John Pudney's poem to the lost airmen, *For Johnny*, which reads:

> Do not despair for Johnny head-in-air,
> He sleeps as sound as Johnny underground.
> Fetch out no shroud for Johnny-in-the-cloud,
> And keep your tears for him in after years.
> Better by far for Johnny-the-bright-star,
> To keep your head and see his children fed.
> (from *Dispersal Point and other air poems*, 1942)

It would be appropriate at this point to mention some of the post-war publications which deal with life on the Home Front. In addition to the official history, *Problems of Social Policy* by R.M. Titmuss, one should also mention *The People's War* by Angus Calder, *How We Lived Then* by Norman Longmate, and *Bombers and Mash* by Raynes Minns. Local publications and local newspapers nationwide are other fruitful sources.

M is for mobilisation or, rather, in this context, the direction of women into essential war work (including the Women's Land Army), which was more completely carried out in Great Britain than in any of the other warring powers – Germany and Russia included. This personal reminiscence illustrates the story of so many women:

My mother, with a husband in the army and three growing children, was one of the many who worked in a factory for the first time. Her work was heavy, hazardous and tiring – she helped make trench mortar bombs. She worked long hours, including night shifts, and was permanently concerned for her husband and her children. Our love for her is matched by our admiration of her. She was one of a remarkable generation of women – perhaps the finest generation of women our country will ever know – and we look upon her, and upon them, with pride.

N is for noted names – the politicians best known to the general public, in addition to Churchill, were Beaverbrook, Anderson, Woolton, Morrison and Bevin, with their vital ministries and with their great power over us. There was also Sir Harold (later, Lord) Mackintosh who was the driving force behind National Savings. There were savings groups in individual streets, hamlets, schools and factories, and their efforts were reinforced by periodic national campaigns for example Warships Week (February 1942), Wings for Victory Week (May 1943), and Salute the Soldier Week (May 1944)

O is for Observer Corps (now Royal).

P is for Purchase Tax (July 1940), the removal of place names to 'confuse' the enemy, post-war credits, the wholesale sacrifice of pots and pans to make Spitfires; German and Italian prisoners of war working on farms, petrol rationing and pool petrol, pig clubs and the malodorous pig-food bins, and, later, food and clothes rationing.

R is for the Royal Ordnance Factories and their 'shadow' factories, and is for Russia – admiration for the Russian people knew no bounds. 'R' is also for the rural areas which were supposed to be safe but which weren't, with their bombs and their aircraft crashes. 'R' is also for the RAF, the Royal Canadian Air Force, the USAAF and for other allied and Dominion squadrons serving with the RAF. The departing squadrons were watched with pride and with prayers. And then there were the railways, grossly overloaded and with deteriorating rolling stock, and which were limited to 30mph.

S is for salvage, shelters (steel, brick; public, private, basement, Anderson and Morrison), Allied servicemen of a dozen or more nationalities, shortages – of things like alarm clocks, linen, books, carpets, wallpaper, razor blades, silk stockings, writing paper and toilet paper – the list was endless, Spam and the other processed meats – Mor, Prem and Tang. Spam, incidentally, stands for 'Supply Pressed American Meat' – so now you know, sixty years on.

T is for travel. Travel of any kind was onerous, with crowded buses, trams and trolley buses, and many public service vehicles were destroyed or damaged in the air raids.

U stands for 'under the counter' and was a by-product of the shortages of non-rationed goods. It was an additional burden for the shopkeepers of the nation who were often accused of favouritism, or worse, by the unlucky customer. 'U' is also for unemployment, the thirties' brand of which was not ended until 1943, when the figure was down to some 60,000.

V is for VE Day and VJ Day, and is also for the immense contribution to the war effort made by the voluntary organisations and services – by the Red Cross, the St John Ambulance Brigade, the (Royal) British Legion, the YMCA and the YWCA, by all the churches, the Boys' Brigade, Scouts and Guides, Army, Air and Sea Cadets, the Women's Junior Air Corps and Girls' Training Corps and, of course, by the (Royal) Women's Voluntary Services. Their duties were legion. The WVS, for example, helped with evacuation, with hospital trains, with the wounded, injured and

Women's Voluntary Service, 'H' District, Greenford, March 1945.

sick in hospitals and with refugees. They fed crews on airfields and civilians in bombed cities, they set up enquiry points after major air raids or raid incidents, and they dealt with the relatives of the casualties – heartrending work. They even made 'Molotov Cocktails' for the Home Guard to hurl at the enemy. They were wonderful and they make a splendid note on which to end these reminiscences.

W is for the women of our land, to whom I have paid due tribute in this book.

X is for xenophobia, which was reduced by the country's shared wartime experience. Large numbers of people experienced overseas travel for the first time and our own islands were awash with strangers.

Y is for youth. The negative impact on many of our young people must be acknowledged. The breakdown of family life, evacuation, absent fathers and working mothers, shortages of every kind, the blackout and bombing all increased delinquency among the young.

Z is for zealot. The war produced conditions in which the zealot could hold sway – on the battle fronts and in the occupied territories. War can truly bring and the best and worst in people.

If you remember any of the above then you must be deep into middle-age or older. But then we have one great consolation over younger readers, for we witnessed at first hand the finest years in our country's long and eventful history.

AFTERWORD

The many war memorials throughout Britain bear mute witness to the appalling military losses in the two world wars, and the annual Remembrance Day parades, large and small, honour the fallen. The 60,000 civilian war dead of the Second World War, however, are seldom commemorated publicly.

Over sixty years ago, the Dean of York Minster spoke of the need for a new kind of war memorial to commemorate the dead of the Second World War. These new memorials, whilst honouring the dead of the armed services, should also, he said, 'honour the men and women who died under the ruins of their own homes and the children who gave their future years so that freedom might flourish in our own and in other countries.'

Remembrance Day parade, Greenford, November 1977.

Mayor Ranjit Dheer at the Remembrance Day Parade in Ealing Green, November 2001.

Mayor, Cllr Ian Potts at the Remembrance Day Parade, Ealing, November 2004.

Over half-a-century later, in 1999, a permanent memorial was unveiled in the churchyard of St Paul's Cathedral to the 30,000 civilian men, women and children and the 2,000 Home Forces personnel who died in London as a result of enemy action and to all who endured the enemy bombardment of the capital. The memorial is in the shape of a polished stone disc and a cap; lies outside the north transept of the cathedral and bears two inscriptions: 'Remember before God the People of London, 1939-1945,' and, 'In war, resolution, in defeat, defiance, in victory, magnanimity, in peace, goodwill.' The cost of the memorial was met by contributors to the *Evening Standard* memorial appeal. This memorial to the people of London, long overdue, is richly deserved.

INDEX

This is not meant to be a comprehensive Index and refers to contributors of information, local places and streets only.

Abernethie's Outfitters 72
Acton Central School 68
Acton Central Station 23
Acton Gazette 23, 78
Acton Green, trenches 23, 49
Acton GWR Station 68
Acton Wells Infant School 24
Acton Old Oak Common Depot 74
Acton Park, VE Day 81
Acton Town Hall 55
Acton Vale allotments 81
Acton, VJ Day 85
Adelaide Road, Southall 62
AEC Factory, Southall 49, 96, 97
Ainsdale Road, Ealing 60
All Saints Road, Acton 54
Alwyn Gardens, Acton 45
Argyle Road, Ealing 33
Avenue, The, Acton 45
Avon Road, Greenford 38
Bartlett, Roy 20, 24, 25, 33, 63
Bayham Road, Acton 54
Beaconsfield Road, Acton 45
Beaumont Road, Acton 45, 57
Bedford Park 66
Beechwood Avenue, Greenford 38
Binmore, Dawn 74
Blandford Road, Acton 45
Blumlein, Alan Dower 91
Boileau Road, Ealing 41
Bollo Bridge Road, Acton 45

Borderston Boys' School, Hanwell 22, 23
Boston Road, Hanwell 44
Braund Avenue, Greenford 38
Brent Valley golf course 60
Brentham 33, 40, 80
Brentham AA 31, 90
Brett, John 72
Bridgeman Road, Acton 45, 50
Broadway, Ealing 57
Bromyard Avenue, Acton 55, 70
Brookfield Road, Ealing 60
Broughton Road, Ealing 41, 66, 70
Burtt, William 69
Cambridge Road, Hanwell 57
Cambridge Road, Southall 49
Carlisle Avenue, Acton 45
Carlton Road, Acton 54
Casualty figures 28, 31, 43, 46, 49, 63, 65
CAV Works, Acton 98
Chalk, Ken 73, 74
Chamberlain Road, VE 82
Chatsworth Gardens, Acton 45
Christ Church, Ealing 57
Chudley, John 72
Church Path, Acton 45
Church Road, Hanwell 60
Church Road, Northolt 95
Churchfield Road, Acton 62
'City of Benares' 23, 40
Clayponds Hospital, Ealing 59
Cleverley Estate 62

Clift, Pauline 89
Cordon, John 82
Cornwall Ave. VJ 85
Costons School 101
Cozens, Tony 69
Creighton Road, Ealing 38
Cuckoo Avenue, Hanwell 58
Darbon, James 54, 55
Dean Gardens, Ealing 23, 40
Deans Road, Hanwell 57
Denison Road, Ealing 60
Drayton Green Road, Ealing 59, 71
Drill Hall, Featherstone Road, Southall 40, 113
Drinkwater, William J. 75, 76
East Acton Baptist Church 57
East Acton Lane 57
Ealing and Old Brentford Burial Board 70
Ealing Broadway Station 21, 23
Ealing Common 33, 40
Ealing Film Studios 109
Ealing Golf Club 47
Ealing Green, VE Day 78
Ealing Museum, Art & History Society 68
Ealing Priory (later Abbey) 41
Ealing Road, Northolt 62
Ealing Savings Campaign 102, 103, 104, 105,
    106, 111, 112
Ealing, VJ Day 85
Eastcote Lane, Northolt 37
Eastham, Eileen 73
Eastmead Avenue, Greenford 38
Eastmead Parade 38
Eccleston Road, West Ealing 72
'Edith' letters 39, 40, 41
Ellerton Road, Ealing 33
EMI factory, Hayes 57, 59
Emmins, Colin 38
Endsleigh Road, Ealing 41
Featherstone School, Southall 71

Fermoy Road, Greenford 37
Fielding Avenue, Acton 45
Fielding Road, Acton 45
First Avenue, Acton 45
Fitzpatrick, Terry 63, 64
Fletcher Road, Acton 54, 55, 57, 66
Ford, Erica 31, 81, 82
Friar's Place Lane, Acton 45
Gladstone Road, Acton 45
Glaxo Factory, Greenford 60, 61
Glencairn Avenue, Ealing 38
Glencairn Drive, Ealing 38
Glenfield Road VE 81
Goodlet, Mr A.K. 16, 20, 26
Green's Stores 40
Greenford 29, 37, 109, 110, 112
Greenford Park Cemetery 33
Greenford, VE Day 82
Gunnersbury Park, A.A 31, 72, 90
Hale Gardens, Acton 55
Hanger Lane, Ealing 21, 60
Hanwell 43, 44, 45, 57
Hanwell Viaduct 49
Harding, Jane 69, 70
Harris, Marjorie 73
Hartington Road, Ealing 48, 59, 70, 71
Haven Green, Ealing 23, 40
Haven Lane, Ealing, VE Day 82
Hearn, John 94, 95
Heath, Mrs M. 49
Heathfield Road, Acton 45
Hereford Road, Acton 45
Hessel Road 51, 83, 93
Higgins, Mr B.J. 70
High Street, Ealing 57, 71
High Street, Southall 49
Holy Trinity Church, Southall 57
Holyoake Walk, Ealing 60
Hoover Factory, Perivale 97, 98

Horn Lane, Acton 45

Horsenden Hill, VE Day 78

Howard Close, Acton 45

Hoylake Road, Acton 45

Jameson, Eileen 71

Jeffries, Mary 70

Jones & Knights shop 48

Keats Way, Greenford 114

Kennedy Road, Hanwell 59

Kent Road, Acton 45, 50

King Edward Memorial Hospital, Ealing 21, 72

Kingfield Road, Ealing 60

Lady Margaret Road, Southall 49

Langford, Beryl 84

Lavington Road, Ealing 40

Lawlor, Ray, Ealing 39

Lewis, Mr and Mrs 74

Leyborne Ave. 42

Lexden Road, Acton 45

Lilley & Skinners, Ealing 71

Little Ealing School 24, 34

Llewellyn's Dairy 74

Load of Hay, Greenford 35

London Transport, Acton Works 99

Long Drive, Greenford 62

Lynton Road, Acton 45, 46, 69

Malden Avenue 57

Mansell, Mrs Alma 68, 69

Mason, Mrs E. 68

Mayfield Road, Acton 46

Mayor of Ealing, Alderman Mrs Taylor 21

Mayor of Ealing, Councillor Lewis 16

Meadvale Road, Ealing 60, 61

Medway Drive, Perivale 34

Middlesex County Times 21, 78, 113

Midland Terrace, Acton 45

Montague Avenue, Hanwell 57

Morland, Mrs 72

Mornington Road, Greenford 38

Mount Avenue, Ealing 31

Mount Park Road, Ealing 32, 33, 56, 62

Napier Factory, Acton 98

Nicholson, Nancy 68, 69, 71

Noble, Barbara 70

Norman Way, Acton 45

Northcote Avenue, Ealing 55, 70

Northfields 40

North Road School, Southall 46

Norwood Rectory, Southall 57

Old Oak Common Lane, Acton 69

Old Oak Road, Acton 45

Osborne Villas, Acton 45

Osterley Park, Home Guard School 91

Palmerston Road, Acton 54

Park Road East, Acton 53

Park Road North, Acton 53, 74

Park Royal 45

Park Royal Road, Acton 59

Park View Road, Ealing 31

Perivale 36, 40, 74

Perryn Road, Acton 45

Peters, Beryl & Keith 38

Pitshanger Lane, Ealing 32, 74, 75

Playhouse Cinema, Greebford 44

Prince's Gardens, Acton 45

Princess Helena College, Ealing 66

Queen's Walk, Ealing 69

RAF Northolt 28, 29

Railway Hotel, Ealing 57, 71

Ravenor Park, VE Day 78

Ravenor School, Greenford 72

Regina Road, Southall 62, 71

Remembrance Parades 122

Rosedene Avenue, Greenford 38

Rothschild Road, Acton 45

Rowdell Road, Northolt 62

Rowse's Stores, Ealing 40

Rugby Road, Acton 57

Ruislip Close 37

Ruislip Road, Greenford 34

Sanders Store 36, 40, 57, 58, 71

Savoy cinema, Acton 114

Second Avenue, Acton 45

Serk Radiators, Park Royal 59

Shaa Road, Acton 45

Shepherds Bush 62

Smith, C. 71

Somerset Road, Acton 54

Sorrell, Keith 49

South Road, Southall 49

Southall Park 57, 113

Southall Salvage 107, 108

Southall Savings 100

Southall, VJ Day/VE Day 79, 80, 85

Southfield Road, Acton 57

Speldhurst Road, Acton 54

Springfield Court, Acton 45

Springfield Gardens, Acton 45

St Alban's Avenue, Acton 54

St Bernard's Hospital, Southall 49, 57

St David's Home, Ealing 39

St John's Church, Ealing 40

St Peter's Church, Ealing 33

St Peter's Road VJ 85

St Saviour's Church, Ealing 41, 46

Staveley Road, Chiswick 54

Stephenson Street, Acton 45

Stockford, Jim 63, 64

Stone, J.M. shop 32

Studland Road, Hanwell 56, 60

Sullivan, Joe 70, 71

Templeman Road, Hanwell 52, 53

Tentelow Lane, Southall 57

The Avenue, Acton 45

The Link, Acton 45

The Vale, Acton 45

Tibbles, Sidney 74

Tudor Road School, Southall 46

Uxbridge Road 58, 59, 60, 66, 71

Valletta Road, Acton 45

Vallis Way, Ealing 34

Verulam Road, Greenford 38

Victoria Road, Acton 45

Voices of Ealing and Hounslow 8

Walpole Park, Ealing 17

Walpole Park, VE Day 78

Waring & Gillow factory 98

Wesley Factory, Acton 45

Wesley Playing Fields, Acton 56

West Acton Infants School 69

Westfield Road 34

'West London Lady' 76

West Middlesex Golf Course 60

Weymouth Avenue 37

Whitton Avenue West, Greenford 57

Willow Road VJ

Windermere Road, Ealing 72

Windmill Lane, Southall 59

Woolworth's, Southall 71

Wormwood Scrubs, AA guns 31, 90, 91

Other titles published by The History Press

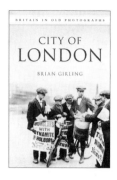

The City of London
BRIAN GIRLING

This book paints the fascinating picture of the events and people, which helped shaped the city we know so well today, including the building and wartime destruction of some of its characteristic features. Focusing on the famous heart of London, most of the images date from the Edwardian period, when London was arguably the greatest city in the world. All the famous city landmarks, such as St Paul's and the Monument, are featured, but equally remarkable are the pictures which show the development of Victorian London.

978-0-7524-4935-7

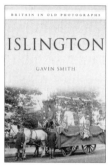

Islington
GAVIN SMITH

This book takes us on a journey through Islington's past, sometimes quite recognizable, sometimes unfamiliar, but in a time of rapid change, it is all the more interesting to look at what has gone before.

978-0-7524-4960-9

Little Book of London
DAVID LONG

Those of us who live in London and love the city (despite all its manifold faults) often have our own list of clandestine destinations, secrets and interesting facts about the capital -- which we're happy to show off to people not lucky enough to live here. But however well you think you know London, the chances are good that that David Long's *The Little Book of London* will enlarge your storehouse of knowledge.

978-0-7509-4800-5

Deal and District At War
DAVID G. COLLYER

Richly illustrated, *Deal and District at War* recounts many unique and controversial events, including a German coastal raid in Sandwich Bay when at least 1 British soldier was snatched; an enemy pilot entertained by a local family after being shot down; cases of smuggling and 'services rendered' by Walmer lifeboat; and the world-famous 'Lifeboat Doctor' James Hall. This book will evoke powerful memories for those who experienced the war and provide fascinating reading for anyone interested in the history of Deal and District.

978-0-7524-4953-1

Visit our website and discover thousands of other History Press books.

www.thehistorypress.co.uk